Outdoor Learning

Outdoor Learning

Past and Present

Rosaleen Joyce

Open University Press

Open University Press
McGraw-Hill Education
McGraw-Hill House
Shoppenhangers Road
Maidenhead
Berkshire
England
SL6 2QL

email: enquiries@openup.co.uk
world wide web: www.openup.co.uk

and Two Penn Plaza, New York, NY 10121–2289, USA

First published 2012

A catalogue record of this book is available from the British Library

ISBN-13: 978-0-33-524301-3 (pb)
ISBN-10: 0-33-524301-0 (pb)
eISBN: 978-0-33-524302-0

Library of Congress Cataloging-in-Publication Data
CIP data applied for

Typesetting and e-book compilations by
RefineCatch Limited, Bungay, Suffolk
Printed and bound in the UK by Bell & Bain Ltd, Glasgow

Fictitious names of companies, products, people, characters and/or data that may be used herein (in case studies or in examples) are not intended to represent any real individual, company, product or event.

The **McGraw·Hill** Companies

I dedicate this book with much love to my first grandchild, Isaac John Patrick Joyce.

Contents

List of tables and figures

Tables

Figures

Acknowledgements

Many thanks to all who supported me in researching and writing this book. Especial thanks to Cathy Nutbrown at Sheffield University for introducing me to publishers. Emma Brennan really got me started with her advice on how to write a book proposal. My friends in POLNET (Promoting Outdoor Learning Network), Diane Wilkinson, Diane Broomhead, Jeanette Gee, Jo Barker, Dawn Trucca, Sue Hayes and Trish Loughlin, have always been there for me. Over the past ten years we have supported one another in keeping outdoor learning alive in the early years. Juliet Robinson has given so much of her time to read and discuss the Forest School chapters. The archivist at the Froebel Archives in Roehampton, Kornelia Cepok, could not have been more helpful, as was Theresa Lane, the head teacher at the Rachel McMillan Nursery School in Deptford. I thank them both for their kind permission to publish the images included in the book.

My many visits to Sweden and the visits of all those I have sent to Sweden to learn about *Skogsmulle* and *I Ur och Skur* have been inspired by the energy and enthusiasm of Magnus and Siw Linde. I am extremely grateful to them for organizing interviews, translating, collecting photographs and, most of all, for becoming such good friends. A huge thank you to Marilyn Barden and Jill Westermark, as well as the team from *Friluftsfrämjandet*, Bo Sköld, Harriet Guter and Helena Graffman, for all the time they gave to interviews, chapter reviews and emails. I learnt so much from Eva, Anna and Sten Frohm about their father, Gösta. I am grateful to them and hope I have done credit to his memory.

Friends and family have been wonderful. The interest from my brothers and sisters in Southampton has been greatly appreciated, particularly in the absence of 'our mum' to talk to. My son and daughter, Sean and Roisin, have kept me going by simply believing I could do it. It is to my husband Pat, however, that I am most indebted. His constant, loving encouragement, support and practical help have made this book possible.

1 Introduction

Outdoor learning has become highly visible in recent years, in the press, in magazines, on television, on the internet, accompanying every advert for a healthy lifestyle and now firmly embedded in the early years curriculum (DfES 2007a). All age groups are involved. Where has this focus come from and what is behind it? Why is this 'discovery' of outdoor learning being presented as something new? My own experience tells me this is not the case. As a child from a very large family in the 1950s I spent a lot of time outside in large groups of all ages, playing with sticks, stones and dirt, largely because there was not enough space to play inside. Children then were expected to amuse themselves while the adults managed the daily chores of everyday life. (See Figures 1.1 and 1.2 for further discussion on this and associated discussion regarding risk.) This leads me to question why these experiences, common to my childhood and that of many others, are considered new today. It also brings to mind a deeper question about how children were perceived at that time. What was the social and political context which framed these views? From a professional perspective, both as an erstwhile practitioner deeply influenced by Swedish Forest School pedagogy and an outdoor play consultant, these questions are of great interest to me.

Much has been written in recent years about how to *be* with children in the outdoors and what to *do* with them, sometimes accompanied by a vague, tokenistic background of the existence of a history of outdoor learning (Jenkinson 2001; Perry 2001; Edgington 2002; Ouvry 2003; Bilton 2004; Banks and Schofield 2005; Garrick 2009). The function of this background seems to be to present outdoor learning as an idealized natural state then and reflect on its absence now. There is some limited discussion as to why this change has occurred, often focusing on fear, litigation and an outcome-driven curriculum (Jenkinson 2001; Edgington 2002; Ouvry 2003). However, Hope et al. (2007) do move the debate forward regarding historical understandings when they consider the historical roots of 'the nature of childhood' in their exploration of 'childhood freedoms and physical activity' (p. 321). From a purely Froebelian

Figure 1.1 Playing out in rural Ireland in 1950

The child on the left of the picture is the author, aged 3 years, playing outside. Her playmate and minder is her sister Ann, who is 4 years old. The space where they played included an open, deep stone quarry just 100 yards from their front door. The plantain or small wood where the women hung the washing was where the children climbed trees, played games and sheltered from the rain. A short path behind them in the picture led down to the busy main road.

Children of all ages played together outside. All were totally free from adult intervention as they played; the fathers were at work and the mothers busy with household chores without the benefit of electricity or running water. All were acutely aware of the boundaries as to where they could and could not play. All were aware of the sanctions. The older children took responsibility for the younger ones and taught them new skills. No one ever fell in the quarry. No one ever went down to the road. This sort of freedom would now be associated with neglect and would involve the Social Services. This sort of freedom is what has undoubtedly shaped the author's views regarding outdoor learning.

perspective, Tovey (2007) also emphasizes the importance of historical under-standings. In looking at the work of Montessori, Froebel, Margaret McMillan, Allen and Isaacs, she describes their ideas and places them in a historical, contemporary context but with no analysis or reference to their own social and political contexts and influences. While Rickinson et al. (2004: 10) acknow-ledge that outdoor learning has a 'long and rich history in the UK' their focus is generally concerned with the 'curriculum' in the form of 'field', 'rural' and 'urban studies'. Their brief description of the 'nature study movement' does

Figure 1.2 Playing 'wee shop'
Playing 'babby house' in the small quarry alongside the big one in front of the author's house was a favourite occupation of her older sister, Sheila. Just like the children in Figure 1.2 she used found pieces of broken china (delft as it was then called) to decorate her play house and spent many happy hours sweeping and keeping the area clean. Risk was not a considered element of such play.

begin to give a wider picture of its historical, social and political context, but their claim that these brief examples demonstrate that many of the current debates about outdoor education are not new is not backed by sufficient evidence and debate on the subject. However, it has to be said that the purpose of their writing was clearly stated as presenting a review of outdoor learning, not an account of its historical significance.

My argument is that most of the existing literature does not address outdoor learning in any real social, political or historical depth. Vincent reinforces my sense of the importance of an historical perspective when he writes about literacy: 'disconnecting . . . from history disables the capacity fully to understand the dynamics of change' (Vincent 2008: 18). My aim is to place a familiar phenomenon, in this case 'outdoor learning', in a theoretical, historical and social context of changing understandings of children and childhood, based on the premise that ideas phase in and out of use depending on social and political contexts. This perspective will enable people to think about how present attitudes developed regarding outdoor learning, where these ideas have come from and whether they are really new ideas. In so doing I hope to provide a new way of looking at this phenomenon.

In the course of this study a consideration of my approach will be followed by a review of the existing literature on outdoor learning, which will suggest the importance of the historical method and its absence in most of the literature. As an exemplification of the historical method in Chapter 2 I will then set outdoor learning in the historical context of childhood to give a broader understanding, while exploring major changes from 1500 to the present day. Chapters 3 to 7 will look at the factors which shaped the views and formation of the pioneers. The major figures I consider are John Amos Comenius (1592–1670), Johann Heinrich Pestalozzi (1746–1827), Friedrich Froebel (1782–1852), Margaret McMillan (1860–1931) and Gösta Frohm (1908–99). Chapter 8 will consider the Forest School in the UK from the 1950s to the present day as one contemporary manifestation of outdoor learning. This is not to deny the existence of other significant pioneers of outdoor learning such as Susan Isaacs, for example, nor does my choice of Forest School suggest this is the only significant, current example of good practice in outdoor learning. My conclusion in Chapter 9 will draw together all of these ideas and discuss how they are taken up and changed in the context of individual political and social environments.

Approach to the study

The historical literature is my data for this study and I rely largely on information from published materials for most of the chapters. The exception to this is Chapter 8 on Gösta Frohm, where there is limited published data. My chosen approach for this chapter involved three face-to-face, informal, semi-structured interviews in Sweden with members of *Friluftsfrämjandet*, the umbrella organization for adult and children's outdoor activities. These interviews were conducted in English with a trusted interpreter present, even though most of the interviewees spoke excellent English. I also followed up leads given by one of the interviewees, Anna Frohm, and subsequently held two very informative telephone conversations with her brother Sten and sister Eva (see referencing section). My aim will be to situate each of my chosen pioneers, historical and contemporary, in terms of the prevailing conceptions of children, childhood and the use of the outdoors, suggesting how these may have influenced their writing and practice. As the study progresses, an exploration of themes which emerge and connect the pioneers will be considered as central to the discussion. These themes will include the topics such as those outlined in Table 1.1.

My rationale for choosing these individuals is that they can be regarded as pioneers of outdoor learning. The way in which they have become pioneers is also the subject of my study. Comenius set the scene for thinking about young

Table 1.1 Themes which link pioneers in this study

The role of	utopianism: seeking a better future through education
The role of	the mother
The role of	the family
The role of	loss, personal and public
The role of	religion
The role of	war and persecution

children as having separate needs from adults and learning through play. He thus shaped Pestalozzi's ideas, which were extended by Froebel.

McMillan took up Froebel's ideas and further developed them. Frohm picked up from his own practice the need to involve younger children in nature, while the Forest Schools in the UK saw a way of connecting nature with the curriculum. All of these pioneers were observing a set of circumstances which, from their contemporary perspectives, made absolute sense. If we start from the present we will see something different. From current perspectives, the views of, for example, Pestalozzi and Froebel have been made the same, but in fact, as will be seen from this study, this view omits their social, political and historical context and is a clear example of 'present-centredness' (Heywood 2001: 13). It may seem obvious to suggest that we all consider history from our present position but it is important to remember that it is the reflexive nature of that position which enables us to step back and gain a new perspective. It is worth noting here that Ariès, the great historian of childhood, made it quite clear that he was trying to understand 'the particularity of the present by comparing and contrasting it with the past' (Ariès 1962: 6). However, in order to do this the particularity of the past had to be replaced with accuracy. Pestalozzi and Froebel's differences have subsequently been edited out of history and it is this sort of exclusion I explore. The pioneers have been chosen because their histories permit the presentation of a clear, historical case study of mutual influence. This illustrates how each pioneer affects the others and how they were influenced in their own time. Finally, I show how they impact on the present.

Before moving on to look at the literature it is necessary to define my terms and explain what I mean by 'outdoor learning' and 'children'. Ranson's general theory of learning sits well with my own vision of what learning is all about, wherever it occurs, when he describes it as 'a process of discovery that generates new understandings about ourselves and the world around us' (1998: 18). Situating this theory in the outdoors clearly defines my view. The definition of a child in the UN convention on the rights of the child (UN 1989) is a person aged between birth and 18 years of age. In this study I am considering the early years of childhood from birth to 8 years of age, a period which is internationally known as 'early childhood' (David and Powell 1999). Detailed definitions of childhood and constructions will be fully explored in Chapter 2.

Review of the literature on outdoor learning: current influences at work

Outdoor learning has been high on the agenda of government policy and documentation over the past decade. The chief factors involved in this are:

- policy making;
- press and public opinion. Everything is now fed by the mass media;
- private business.

Policy making

The *Curriculum Guidance for the Foundation Stage* (CGFS) introduced by the Qualifications and Curriculum Authority (QCA) in 2000 was the first real example of the government making a commitment to outdoor learning, advocating 'carefully planned and purposeful activity that provides opportunities for teaching and learning . . . Well-planned play both indoors and outdoors is a key way in which young children learn with enjoyment and challenge' (QCA 2000: 11–25). Prior to this there was no emphasis on outdoor learning in the documentation and guidelines of *Early Learning Goals* (QCA 1999), *Desirable Outcomes for Children's Learning* (DfEE/SCAA 1996) or the Rumbold Report, *Starting with Quality* (DES 1990). Some suggestions were made for activities such as seasonal and sensory walks, for example, but weather observations were, more often than not, made from the inside of classrooms. In 2002 the Department for Education and Skills (DfES) published *Birth to Three Matters*, placing the youngest children firmly at the centre of the environments in which they were being cared for, with recommendations that they also use the outdoors as well as the indoors. No clear definitions of outdoor learning were described at this stage in either the CGFS or *Birth to Three Matters*.

However, this all changed again in 2007 when the DfES combined CGFS (2000) and *Birth to Three Matters* (2002) with *The National Standards for Under-eights Day Care and Childminding* (DfES 2003c), to create a new statutory framework called *The Early Years Foundation Stage* (EYFS). This framework acknowledged outdoor learning wholeheartedly as playing a vital role in the education and care of birth to 5-year-old children and made it an entitlement, stating that 'all early years providers must have access to an outdoor play area which can benefit the children' or, if they didn't have access to their own outdoor space, 'they must make arrangements for daily opportunities for outdoor play in an appropriate location' (DfES 2007a: 7). In September 2008 this became mandatory for all early years providers. This included 'all maintained schools; non-maintained schools; independent schools and childcare registered by Ofsted on the Early Years Register . . .' (DfES 2007a: 8). Outdoor learning was now a clear expectation for all children of registered providers.

Practitioners were urged by government to 'value the outdoors as much as the indoors' in an attempt to raise the standards of underachieving boys (DCSF 2007a: 18). At the same time they were encouraged to use the outdoors since children who speak English as an additional language 'tend to be less inhibited in their language use in the outdoor environment (DCSF 2007b: 13). Even the much talked about teaching of phonics in the early years found a place for itself in the outdoors (DfES 2007b: 2).

The EYFS came about as part of the government's ten-year childcare strategy aimed at halving child poverty by 2010 and eradicating it by 2020 (DCSF 2007c; Oppenheim and Lawton 2009). HM Treasury (HMT) published this ten-year plan, *Choice for Parents, the Best Start for Children* (2004), which was in turn under the umbrella of a green paper, *Every Child Matters* (DfES 2003b). This green paper and the subsequent Education Act of 2004 were set up as a response to Lord Laming's report on safeguarding children following the tragic death of 3-year-old Victoria Climbie in 2002 (Pugh 2006).

Press and public opinion

All this legislation can be viewed against a backdrop of growing fear for children's safety (Edgington 2002). The murder of two schoolgirls in 2002 in Soham added to this fear of allowing children to be outside without adult protection. It also raised the question of trust in professional systems for monitoring those who work with children, resulting in further safeguarding guidelines (Roche and Tucker 2007). High-profile child abductions in the media such as that of Madeleine McCann increased this fear for children's safety. Alerting parents to the latest satellite tracking device (showcased at the Electronics Show in Las Vegas), *The Guardian* (Johnson, 12 January 2009) reassured parents that now they will always know where their children are. Sadly for many children, the school playground became, or has become, the only place where they play outside (White 2004; DfES 2006b). These and other fears of 'stranger danger' increased traffic, risk and potential for litigation have led parents and educators to keep their children indoors or only outside when supervised or accompanied by an adult (Edgington 2002; Rickinson et al. 2004; Maynard 2007a).

Fear of the consequences of a generation of children being 'reared in captivity' (O'Hara 2007), forever under the supervisory adult eye, led to a shift in popular and government thinking towards a more creative curriculum (DfES 2003a; Waite and Rea 2006). A rise in the development of agencies promoting outdoor learning also reflected a reaction against this period of relentless change and increased regulation. In 2006 the DfES supported and published the views of a wide range of people from all walks of life, who put themselves forward to pledge support for taking learning outside the classroom. This resulted in *Learning Outside the Classroom Manifesto* (DfES 2006a), a document which supports outdoor learning as a vehicle for improving educational outcomes by engaging children in meaningful first-hand experiences. This approach is echoed in the growing number of Forest Schools, whose holistic focus takes particular account of the personal growth of the individual in terms of self-esteem and self-worth. Central to this pedagogy is responsible risk taking, which is seen as a feature underpinning all learning, a feature which is notably absent in the prevailing litigious culture of fear (Davis et al. 2006). Nielsen (2008) warns against adopting the example of the Norwegian approach to outdoor learning as a cure-all for today's ills. She argues that the Norwegian approach is culturally specific and not readily transferable. Being outdoors is 'an important part of being Norwegian' and children are seen as 'bearers of national culture' (p. 54). Louv's updated book *Last Child in the Woods* supports the growing fear of children losing touch with nature and the development in America of campaigns such as 'Leave no child inside' (2008: 351). In her article 'Young children, environmental education, and the future', Davis (1998) high-lights her real concerns for a future peopled by adults with no knowledge or experience of the outdoors.

There are other fears related to these 'alternative' outdoor learning approaches. Maynard and Waters (2007), in their research on a group of early years teachers in South Wales, found that they were using the same adult-led pedagogical approaches outside as traditionally used inside. Maynard and Waters believe that the rationale for this approach focuses on the outdoors as not being seen as relevant to their role as teachers where all the 'real' teaching takes place in the classroom. As a practitioner, my concern was for the shivering, slow-moving 3-year-old who regarded the outdoor environment as dangerous and inhospitable. What was the motivation for insisting that he or she had this experience? Did that child benefit in the long term from being outside when he or she would have been much happier, in the short term, if left inside in the warm?

Wood (2007: 312) argues that 'provision for young children is now situated at the centre of wider social policy frameworks such as health, social care, workforce development'. A consequence of this is the current emphasis on obesity in children and the physical nature of outdoor learning being featured as a potential antidote (DCSF 2007c). There is also a commitment from the *Children's Plan* (DCSF 2007c) to a national play policy for England (DCSF and DCMS 2008), and a new early years framework for Scotland which states that 'outdoor play in particular can . . . be a major contribution to outcomes around obesity' (Scottish Government 2008: 18). It is worth noting that the Welsh Assembly Government was already *implementing* their play policy in 2006. In Northern Ireland the *Playboard: Fit for Play Quality Award* scheme argues that outdoor play programmes which combine 'physical activity and nutrition' will help tackle the 'obesity crisis' (Environmental Education Forum 2008: 8). Akdag and Danzon (2006: 4) of The World Health Organization Europe add weight to this view stating that 'childhood obesity is one of the most serious public health challenges of the twenty-first century', taking this argument into the realms of socio-economic development and inequality. They place full responsibility on governments to create 'a portfolio of interventions designed to change the social, economic and physical environment so as to favour healthy lifestyles' (Akdag and Danzon 2006: 4).

Government legislation in the UK is confronting these issues, respecting children and young people's UNCRC (1989, article 12) right to be consulted about matters that concern them, hopefully leading to increased opportunities for them to play outside safely and, in so doing, increase their opportunities to have a healthier way of life (DCSF 2008).

Private business

The growth in the private sector of early years provision has created a new phenomenon: early years settings as businesses competing in an ever-increasing market. Moss (2007) questions the ambiguity of their position, arguing that the business ethic is incompatible with early childhood values such as democracy. Furthermore, a development of monopolies, such as the Australian ABC group which holds a large chunk of the market in Australia, New Zealand, America and the UK, has led to a 'universalization' of ethos, practice and even furniture, regardless of the cultural context of these settings, in turn leading to a potential erosion of the diversity of child contexts and childhoods (Hinton 2008: 296; Newberry 2008: 2; Pence and Nsamenang 2008: 1). Moss (2009: viii–2) refers to these establishments as 'factories for producing predetermined outcomes . . . [and] hegemonic globalization', a market model discourse which, in his view, denies plurality, an ingredient central to any debate on early childhood education. This globalized, corporative approach to provision dominated the field from 2001. ABC went into receivership in 2008, selling off many of its centres to cover costs, leaving thousands of children without provision. The shortcomings of the market model were apparent to all.

Another accompanying feature of early years provision as a business is the industry which has rapidly developed selling state of the art outdoor equipment designed to ensure each child is working towards and achieving the EYFS early learning goals. This industry is prospering and frequently results in settings filling their outdoor areas with expensive equipment in order to compete in the market. Ouvry (2003) argues that they are missing the point regarding the central importance of outdoor learning, which does not depend on the volume and expense of the equipment but rather on 'the capacity of what is there to be noticed by the children (and adults), to capture their imagination and curiosity so they want to look further' (Ouvry 2003: 34). Tovey supports this argument, suggesting there is a real danger that these 'increasingly prepackaged' spaces eliminate 'the odd corners, niches, nooks and crannies, which we know provide endless fascination for children's play [and learning]' (2007: 58).

My own position regarding outdoor learning is that it enables children to have greater freedom, in a healthier environment, to learn, manage risk and problem solve in a meaningful way. Rose (1992) warns that this freedom comes at a price in our current audit culture where accountability is central: 'This very freedom [becomes] a form of governance subject to rules of conduct . . . leading to structures to administer this . . . these practices are governed through freedom' (p. 215). Governance of outdoor learning therefore requires rules and regulations for 'responsible risk taking', for example so that it can be audited. It is, however, the inevitable relationships of power within these structures which we need to be aware of if we are to enable children to be free. These include, adult–child, child–adult and child–child relationships as well as the relationship the child has with the outdoor environment itself (MacNaughton 2005). Reflexive practitioners who are aware of these structures and inherent relationships will act responsibly and intelligently in their use of the outdoors (Faubion 1994).

Understanding present developments in a historical context

Is the high degree of governance of early childhood education perhaps partly responsible for the fear adults feel about letting their children go out to play unsupervised? Have these adults become disempowered by all this regulation? On the one hand they are being told they have choice and responsibility: 'We recognize that children are brought up by parents, not by government' (DCSF 2008: 4). On the other they are being told how to exercise that choice and responsibility (HMT 2004). Does the child have a voice when it comes to choice, if only the opportunity to choose between an outdoor or indoor environment (Nutbrown 2006: 155–8; Hinton 2008; James and James 2008: 28)? Yet, the reciprocal nature of this policy and political intervention cannot be overlooked since the policy makers can also be seen to be simply keeping up to date with what they perceive to be going on out there in the public sphere.

However, all these questions and choices of the present are the result of historical developments. The emphasis on the necessity for understanding present developments in a historical context is the chief argument of the book. Our perspective needs to be long-term as well as short: the past decade is a product of the decades immediately before, but these preceding years are themselves only truly understandable if we see that they too are just the expression of cumulative changes that have taken place over hundreds of years. Each generation builds on the previous one, forgets it has done so, and thus fails to fully understand itself and its times. With this in mind I now move on to Chapter 2 to look at outdoor learning in terms of its immediate social context of understandings of childhood, and then examine how these understandings have changed since 1500.

2 Outdoor learning in the historical context of childhood, 1500 to the present

Factors for change in the early modern period from 1500 to 1750 and the late modern period from 1750 to the present

This chapter begins by looking at the major forces for change in the early modern period (1500–1750) followed by a brief discussion of factors evident in the late modern period (1750 to the present). It considers how these influences may have shaped contemporary conceptions of children, childhood and the outdoors. It is clear from the literature that the concepts of children and childhood do vary over time . . . 'They differ across time; they differ within their own time' (Cunningham 2006: 13–14). For instance, in the early eighteenth century Locke saw childhood as a preparation for adulthood and the child as a *tabula rasa,* a blank slate, while Montessori in the twentieth century chastised adults who viewed the child as 'something empty' (Montessori 1966: 16). In the seventeenth century the child was perceived as 'evil', and as 'innocent' in the Romantic period (Cunningham 2006: 13–14). Maynard (2007a) argues that the current view is that children are 'vulnerable and in need of protection' (p. 390), while Wyness (2006) sees childhood as a time of simplicity and innocence usually associated with play and freedom from responsibility.

The history of childhood is often thought to be a history of progress exemplified by the introduction of compulsory education in 1880 and the post-war welfare state (Cunningham 1995, 2006; Corsaro 1997). However, Ariès (1962) did not see life improving for children over time, whereas De Mause (1974) did, arguing that things have steadily improved for children, as the further back in time you went the 'lower the level of childcare' (1974: 1). 'Childhood' is often seen as an inevitable progression from birth to adulthood but Postman (1994) suggests that when regarded historically and as a social construction its

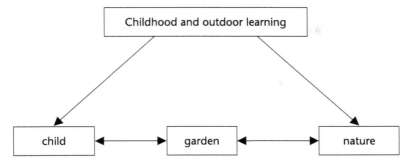

Figure 2.1 Links between constructions of childhood and outdoor learning

existence can no longer be seen as inevitable. Because adults often see themselves as specialists when thinking about children, if only because they have shared an experience of being children themselves, this makes it all the more important to challenge our assumptions through an examination of the major historical changes in views of childhood and how these influenced opinion at the time. My task is also to examine understandings of outdoor learning historically. How best to link my twin concerns, childhood and outdoor learning? Figure 2.1 helps to do so in what I think is a revealing way.

Ideas of nature and the child are linked historically by the garden. The garden has been a crucially significant interface between the child and nature. This will be explored and examined more fully in Chapters 4 to 6 when looking at Pestalozzi, Froebel and McMillan's approach to outdoor learning. The garden is a particularly powerful place to explore since in most cultures this is where nature/nurture and nature/culture meet.

While there is little doubt that the first attempts to impose order on the landscape were inspired by the need for food, the inclination to tame nature has a long and continuous history. Conran and Pearson go on to explain that this mastery of nature is evident from the earliest times in:

> . . . the peristyle gardens of Syracuse and Alexandria in the first century BC, continuing through to the gardens of Roman villas and the cloistered monastery gardens of mediaeval Europe to the French baroque and the English Landscape movements of the eighteenth century and beyond.
>
> (Conrad and Pearson 1998: 12)

Over time the garden has been represented in many different ways and in turn represents many different things. The Garden of Eden from which Adam and Eve were expelled was portrayed in religion as a place of temptation and potential evil. By the Renaissance the garden had became a space for pleasure and the enjoyment of nature. The Gardens of Versailles express the absolutist state power of the monarchy (Mukerjii 1997). The eighteenth-century garden expresses the political outlook of the liberal Whig aristocracy by representing nature as a form of liberty, allowing nature to express itself as a form of freedom. Examples of this can be seen in William Kent's (1685–1748) design for the gardens at Chiswick House (1734) and the work of Lancelot Brown, more commonly known as Capability Brown (1716–83), who modelled his gardens on the harmonies of nature, such as the one at Blenheim Palace. These harmonies represented the ideas of political equilibrium under Whig aristocratic leadership in a 'balanced' constitution (Conran and Pearson 1998). The nineteenth-century garden is, for instance, represented by gardens in parks. These public gardens expressed the management of class relations in the new conditions of urbanization and industry (Joyce 2003).

Turning now to concepts of childhood, Ariès (1962) suggests that the modern concept of childhood did not exist in the Middle Ages. Neither too did the concept of 'outdoor learning'. In defining the concept of childhood, he highlights its absence: 'It corresponds to an awareness of the particular nature of childhood, that particular nature which distinguishes the child from the adult . . . in mediaeval society this awareness was lacking' (p. 125). Ariès believed that beyond infancy children were treated as small adults. Scholars across many disciplines acknowledge Aries's contribution to the debate on childhood as a social construction (Postman 1994; Corsaro 1997; Goldson 1997; Cunningham 2006; Wyness 2006; James and James 2008). Postman (1994) agrees with Ariès's assertion that childhood did not become apparent until the sixteenth century but sees its emergence as an outcome of the invention of the printing press. He believed that this invention made visible the difference between adults and children in terms of literacy competence. This separation of adults from children is an important shift in understandings of childhood constructions. Ariès's call to historians to take childhood seriously has generated a lot of interest, not just among historians, but also social scientists, demographers and philosophers. These disciplines had hitherto seen the role of children and childhood as part of their research and practice concerned with the family and education.

Hanawalt (1993) disputes Ariès's idea, arguing that the concept of childhood did exist and that families in the Middle Ages were aware of children as separate beings who required different treatment from adults. She shows how they stayed with their mother until the age of 7 and were then gradually introduced into the world of work, the boy following his father's line of work and the girl being largely concerned with the domestic duties of the home. In arguing her case Hanawalt (1993) illustrates activities that children engaged in: 'Children were wandering around and playing games such as walking on logs or playing ball with friends' (p. 66).

She also suggests that children were agents in their own lives and not simply controlled by adults:

> [They] played ball, tag, ran races, played hoops, and imitated adult ceremonies such as royal entries, masses and marriages. Some celebrations were just for children ... the most notable being the 'boy bishops' where they swapped roles with adults who then had no authority over them and their autonomy was celebrated in a very public fashion.
>
> (Hanawalt 1993: 54)

Cunningham (1995: 1) would argue, however, that Hanawalt is failing to make a necessary distinction here between her observations of children's behaviours and an awareness of childhood as 'a shifting set of ideas'. The consequence of this is that although we gain valuable insight through her narratives as to how children lived and played outdoors in the Middle Ages, this in itself does not constitute a contemporary concept of childhood.

During this period, most children did not go to school, although the number of schools was on the increase at the end of the fourteenth century, since many guilds required literacy as a prerequisite to apprenticeships (Hanawalt 1993). This education only applied to boys since girls were excluded from schooling at the time, and indeed subsequently (Wyness 2006). Until education became compulsory in the late nineteenth-century children had to pay fees to attend school, so education was a limited option for the poor. The structure of the nuclear family as we recognize it today was only beginning to develop and the majority of children worked as part of the extended family economy.

Hobhouse (2002: 100) informs us that any sense of the classical idea of using the countryside as a source of 'comfort and beauty' had disappeared altogether in the Middle Ages. Paintings from this time emphasize this point by depicting formal gardens surrounded by high walls to keep the wildness of nature at bay. The actual environment of the urban outdoors was, according to Hanawalt, physically dangerous with '. . . crowded living conditions and prevalent filth ... inhospitable to children, who played freely in streets running with raw sewage' (1993: 67). Little was done at this time to protect children from these life-threatening risks. The power of the church was a central governing influence on everyday lives at a local level (Cunningham 1995). The church influenced opinion by portraying the surrounding countryside as a dangerous, evil space where, '. . . the ancient pagan gods lurking in the forest were not only dangerous but evil spirits akin to the devil, who could seduce a man from his Christian beliefs' (Hobhouse 2002: 100). Although this fear of the natural world still exists today its influence is no longer based on religion. One of the main forces for change in attitudes to children and childhood in the early modern period (1500–1750) was in fact the church. The others were the state and educational ideas and practice. I shall now consider these in turn.

The church

The first factor for change in this period is religion. This dominated attitudes to children in the sixteenth and seventeenth centuries, a period marked by civil wars and disturbances. Where Catholicism had been the main influence on children in the Middle Ages in northern and Eastern Europe this was now replaced by Protestantism. In Protestant England in the seventeenth century, Protestants and especially Puritans agonized over the state of children's souls. Cunningham (2006) argues that present-day parental anxiety in the UK about the dangers of the outdoors can be equated with this period of concern for children's souls. The stain of original sin, a legacy of Adam and Eve's failure to obey God's wishes in the Garden of Eden, acknowledged by Catholics but cleansed by the sacrament of baptism, was not so easily eradicated in the Protestant mind. Despite reform and rationalism, old ideas remained. Children were perceived as 'evil', and parents and schoolmasters began to impose a strict disciplinary regime to enable them to overcome their nature and develop the self-control seen as a characteristic of adulthood (Postman 1994). This concept echoes the mediaeval clergy's notion of nature and the natural world as full of evil, pagan gods and spirits in the forest tempting man away from his religion.

The state

Secondly, there was the emergence of a new kind of state, which, much more directly than hitherto, involved schemes for the governance of territory and population. Because of this, new kinds of knowledge and expertise became necessary. These involved the education of the upper classes in the governance both of themselves and of the population generally (Blanning 2000). Therefore the increasing equation of the family and the state became apparent and with it a new concern for the education of the child in the virtues that could be of use to the state (Cunningham 2006).

In the Renaissance of fifteenth-century Florence, in upper-class families, children were regarded as central to the future success of the state. The family was seen to be a prototype of the state and since, the state was ruled by men, the father had a central role in creating harmonious relationships which would be reflected in state virtues (see Figure 2.2). This was an important shift away from the mediaeval practice of women having responsibility for childrearing until the age of 7.

Figure 2.2   The Renaissance father (Lorenzo de Medici) as the head of the family

With the advent of the printing press Florentine advice books began to appear and upper-class adults began to become literate. Early learning was now recommended and this too became the responsibility of the father 'teaching children their letters soon after weaning' (Cunningham 1995: 43). These ideas spread to other parts of Europe and at the turn of the century Erasmus wrote a series of pamphlets and books on how to educate children. These would, however, have been the children of the wealthy, and invariably boys. Cunningham goes on to illustrate how the writing of Erasmus echoed the Florentine advice books' suggestion that education should begin early. A child 'ought to imbibe . . . with the milk that he suckles, the nectar of education', for 'he will most certainly turn out to be an unproductive brute unless at once and without delay he is subjected to a process of intensive education' (1995: 43). This was a new attempt to reshape the child into a rational being. However, the long-standing Protestant emphasis on the sinfulness of the child continued. This combination of old and new in fact has marked all historical times. Even in the period of Rousseau's conception of the child as a rational innocent being, older notions regarding the inherent evil in children were all just below the surface. These double images in fact persist into the present. For example, the child today is viewed as an 'innocent monster' and childhood as 'monstrous innocence', particularly in relation to the high-profile media cases of child murder.

The emergence of the Italian Renaissance garden reflected the new emergence of the secular state. Such gardens represented cosmic order and the capacity of humans to mirror this order by perfecting nature in the shape of the carefully executed garden (Hobhouse 2002). Using 'new found rules of mathematics and perspective', the early Renaissance builders created gardens where 'art and nature could co-exist . . . the garden outside was an architectural extension of the inside' (Hobhouse 2002: 120–1). Both inside and outside gardens came to represent political order and were no longer enclosed and inward looking as in mediaeval times. They began to look outwards, acknowledging the potential order and beauty of nature while celebrating its delights. Renaissance man was encouraged to participate in these delights. The garden was now a place for 'outdoor living, social pleasures and philosophical debates' (Hobhouse 2002: 125).

Education

The third factor for change in the early modern period was education. Erasmus wrote about how boys could regulate their lives to overcome innate evil but he abhorred the corporal punishment often accompanying these practices (Cunningham 2006). This view of children as evil beings continued to dominate understandings of children into the seventeenth century. Nonetheless, Ariès (1962), Postman (1994) and Valentine (2004) all regard this as the time when childhood emerged as a distinct concept, children being defined as different in kind from adults. Postman, as we have seen, relates this to the technology which separated children from adults in terms of literacy competence. Ariès argues that the real factors for change during this period were 'the scholastic reformers of the fifteenth century, Cardinal d'Estouteville, Gerson, the organizers of the colleges and pedagogicas, and finally and above all the Jesuits, the Oratatorians and the Jansenists in the seventeenth century' (1962: 317).

Developments in the wake of the scientific revolution in the seventeenth century, emphasizing the importance of first-hand knowledge, were to have a profound influence on understandings of first-hand experience in the education of children. Comenius (1592–1670), the powerful and influential educational philosopher, recommended sensory experiences as opposed to rote learning (Bowen 1981). (His life will be explored in the following chapter.)

Unlike Bacon, however, he believed in a holistic approach to education whereby the intellect engaged with the senses, both spiritually and emotionally. This approach to education remains a central element of indoor and outdoor educational theories today. In England the seventeenth century gave rise to scientific empiricism, which was important in heralding the idea that all knowledge is based on first-hand experience. These ideas were above all developed by the 'experimental philosopher' Francis Bacon (1561–1626). The debt of current approaches to learning in the early years is obvious, particularly outdoor learning and the Forest School experience (Ouvry 2003; Rickinson et al. 2004; Davis et al. 2006; DfES 2007a; Tovey 2007; Louv 2008).

In the late modern period, from 1750 to the present, religion was less significant though still important. The state and the place of education continued to be significant, of course, but both were now in large part responding to the new industrialization and urbanization that marked Western Europe and the USA. I will consider these main forces at work, beginning with the state. During the early part of this period Britain was embroiled in wars and revolutions across Europe. The nature of 'the state' changed dramatically. The *laissez-faire* state in Britain between 1820 and the First World War regulated society and the economy in line with what was believed to be their 'natural' operations. These should be allowed to function according to their own laws without interference. There was, however, a strong element of moral intervention in the form of Poor Laws, which were designed to deter idleness and the vices it was assumed to foster (Thompson 1990). This form of governance gradually gave way towards the end of the nineteenth century to greater government intervention in education and policies of social welfare. The health and welfare of the poor became central to educational reform. This was designed to improve Britain's efficiency in the military, government, economic and social sectors. It was in fact a bid to redress the prevailing situation in which Britain was being outstripped in trade and industrial production by other countries. As Britain industrialized and urbanized, the state became increasingly involved in the organization of education, the size of the population increasing enormously (Roberts 1996). Education became compulsory in the UK in 1880 but only became free in 1891; it became compulsory much earlier in Prussia, in 1810, and in 1882 in France. US compulsion followed slowly after, in 1852.

Bowen (1981) notes that as anti-clerical movements grew across Europe more rational forms of religious belief also spread. In the UK and US, rational religion was also evident, in the form of rationalist Protestantism (for example, Quakerism and Unitarianism). Religion therefore still shaped education and resulted in many attempts across Europe to find alternatives to the dogmatism of established religious practice. Up until the twentieth century, however, the state in the UK remained relatively decentralized and relied heavily on the voluntary principle and philanthropy. Nonetheless, with increasing force from the 1890s, Britain was similar to the other major nations of Europe in the commitment of the state to universal educational provision. With this commitment went the need to decide when, where and how the child should be taught. This interventionist tone was accented much further by the need to fight two world wars. In the name of the national interest, education and health became regulated by the state in a bid to create healthier citizens for the future. Resulting regulation by the new Liberal governments of the early twentieth century included the introduction of free school meals, a school medical service in 1907 and a Children's Act in 1908. Children now became 'symbols of social hope, of a better and healthier future, of individuality and selfhood' (Steedman 1990: 198). As has been seen in the Introduction, a new welfare state emerged from 1900 to 1970. From 1970 to the present, however, the market has become the chief model for educational organization, in line with the neo-liberal direction of politics and the economy. It will already be amply evident how destructive this has been educationally.

By the mid-nineteenth century we see the emergence of education as a science and the concomitant growth of 'experts' in the field. No longer satisfied with religious explanations of the world, new questions began to be asked by philosophers, the new 'educationalists' and scientists alike, challenging conventional assumptions. As governments sought to reorganize and rebuild their nations after the wars and revolutions of 1789 to 1830 they looked to education as the principal means of doing this and sought theories of education that would meet their requirements (Bowen 1981). At the same time new approaches to thinking about education as a science began to gain ground during the Enlightenment. Thinkers such as Jean-Jacques Rousseau and John Locke began to influence practice. Their work heralded the beginning of a new, modern invention of childhood. This was taken up and developed by Pestalozzi, Froebel and McMillan. By the early twentieth century the emergence of the new 'science' of psychology together with psychoanalytic theories began to have an effect on education. Donald Winnicott (1896–1971) and Erik Erikson (1902–94), for instance, became influential at different times and in different ways. Winnicott's work highlighted the importance of the mother–child relationship. His theories on mother–child interaction and the role of transitional objects in helping the child separate from the mother became and remain central to good practice. Erikson's hypothesis was based on stages of development, which covered a whole life span, as opposed to the Piaget model, which ended at adolescence (Pound 2005).

As will be seen in Chapters 4 and 5, Pestalozzi and Froebel picked up on the negative impact of mass education and worked to counter this while also seeking to develop education as a science. They supported the notion that the child was an innocent individual who needed nurturing and guidance, following as they did the utopian, Enlightenment view that education was essential for the redemption of mankind. McMillan addressed state concern with the impact of industrialization and urbanization on the health of young children.

Concepts of childhood are not just about time; they are also about place. In traditional Confucian China, for example, children were seen as miniature adults. Bai (2005) argues, however, that children became active agents in separating themselves from adults in much the same way as the mediaeval 'boy bishops' described by Hanawalt earlier in this chapter. By adding imagination to their playful imitation of adult activities, 'this imitation became a form of creative activity that . . . marked their identity' (2005: 28). Therefore they were not simply inactive participants in their own cultural legacy; nonetheless, that legacy shaped the conditions for their own active agency, so that this activity did not take place in a vacuum. Confucian notions of childhood still determined their role in the wider scheme of things, in that childhood was seen to involve subjection to parents and authority in general, as well as that of the state. This is only one example of cultural and geographical variation, which is also, of course, historical variation, in that traditional Confucian ideas were themselves not unchanging.

However, it is historical change that I am concerned with here, so I will now move on to an examination of the great educational thinker, Comenius.

Reflective question

Consider the following question individually or in a group:

- How will your knowledge of the main factors for change in the early modern period and the late modern period inform your current practice?

3 Born to be educated: John Amos Comenius (1592–1670)

Education and society in the time of Comenius

Figure 3.1 John Amos Comenius

John Amos Comenius (1592–1670), the philosopher and theologian, can be seen as the father of early childhood education. I have chosen Comenius as a starting point for my discussion on outdoor learning, past and present, since he was the first to promote the idea that children learn through play. It is on the basis of his ideas that all subsequent notions of children and play both indoors and outdoors are based. However, the notion of 'outdoor learning' did not exist in his time and did not really come into common usage until the late-nineteenth and early twentieth-century with the development of groups such as the Scouting Movement. Comenius did nonetheless advocate the outdoor world of nature as a model for educational reform. This will be explored more fully in the section illustrating the implementation of his ideas. His holistic approach to learning through the senses remains the cornerstone of educational theory and practice today. This chapter argues that new ideas such as these do not appear in a vacuum. They grow out of the political, social and cultural climate of the time. What were the major factors that would have influenced his formation, theory and practice?

Comenius emerged at the beginning of the Age of Reason, a period which rejected religious explanations of the world and looked for more scientific evidence for arguments, a view often underpinned by the contemporary utopian assumption that there was a better world to create (Bowen 1981). The child was regarded in the seventeenth century as inherently evil and in need of control. Comenius believed, however, that there was an inherent good within the child that could be brought out by education and a more lenient approach to discipline. Methods of instruction at the time were extremely harsh and corporal punishment was the norm. Michel de Montaigne (1533–92), as cited in Bowen (1981: 79), attacked these school regimes, suggesting that if we truly cared about children we would keep them away from schools altogether and just allow them to play. He condemned the inherent violence and unsuitability of the teaching methods, wishing instead that 'classrooms could be hung with festoons of flowers rather than, as they are, with blood-soaked birches'. Clauser (1961) claims that Luther's treatment at the hands of schoolmasters was testament to this when he was beaten fifteen times in one day, and any tendency towards milder forms of disciplining was regarded with great suspicion.

Comenius advocated that all people should be educated. At a time when education was exclusive to the wealthy it is significant that Comenius took this radical position regarding universal education. Until then education had been largely dominated by mediaeval procedures based on Aristotelian principles within a comprehensive system of Western philosophy, which brought together logic and science, politics and metaphysics, as well as morality and aesthetics. European schools were no longer satisfied with explanations of the world based on these principles, particularly with regard to cosmology and man's place in it. Comenius later went on to fully describe his position on universal education in *Didactica Magna*, which was published in Amsterdam in 1658.

Bowen (1981) argues that the scientific revolution in the seventeenth century stimulated a movement of questioning and reform leading to a new doctrine of empiricism initiated by Francis Bacon, as mentioned in the previous chapter. Bowen goes on to say that Bacon believed he had found a new way of talking about the world. This he described as a new inductive logic which grew out of sensory experiences which could observe and record the facts of nature in all its detail and so provide an exact knowledge. Bacon saw this as a more rational and efficient way of interpreting the world. His views strongly influenced educational reformers of the seventeenth century. Comenius's emphasis on learning through sensory experience rather than the traditional rote learning of his time is a clear illustration of this. This approach to learning is an integral part of good outdoor practice today.

The church strongly opposed this philosophy, seeing its hitherto unchallenged view of science as an aspect of natural theology being brought into question. In addition to this, by the end of the sixteenth century a growing class of landed gentry and urban bourgeois were already making demands for secular education. This situation, coupled with the ongoing intransigence of the church and the narrowness of the university curriculum, led to the formation of voluntary societies and institutions, outside the universities, dedicated to scientific and humanist research as well as promoting the common good (Sadler 1966; Bowen 1981). The first of these appeared in Italy in the early seventeenth century and the Royal Society was founded in England in 1662. These developments led to an increase in scientific and philosophical communication internationally through journals such as the *Journal des Savants* and *Philosophical Transaction* (Husen 2003). Educational reformers such as Samuel Hartlib (1600–62), Comenius and Bacon were all working on a basis of cross-national co-operation and sharing of ideas. Serious attempts were being made during this time to make the links between the newly gained scientific knowledge and the process of education.

Husen (2003) argues that an expanding knowledge of the world and major advances in technology added weight to new, emerging questions surrounding nature and creation. For example, Galileo, a contemporary of Comenius, was branded a heretic by the Inquisition of 1633 for daring to question Aristotelian philosophy by suggesting that natural science could be separated from moral philosophy. Other contemporaries, such as the French humanists and educational reformers Pierre de la Ramee (1515–72) and Francois Rabelais (1495–1553), were also pushing the boundaries of how the world was perceived. Rabelais's inclusion of the study of the natural world in his educational programmes marks a significant shift in thinking from the traditional humanist focus on literacy. This inclusion of the natural world in educational theory and practice could also be seen as a possible starting point for thinking about learning in and from the outdoors. Nature is here perceived as 'good'. Bowen cites Rabelais:

> A knowledge of nature is indispensable . . . let there be no sea, river or fountain but you know the fish that dwell in it. Be familiar with all the shrubs, bushes and trees in forest or orchard, all the plants, herbs and

flowers that grow on the ground, all the birds of the air, all the metals in the bowels of the earth, all the precious stones in the orient and the south. In other words be well informed in everything that concerns the physical world.

(Bowen 1981: 30)

All of these figures can be seen as part of a wider seventeenth-century European shift towards educational reform in a bid to counter the dominant features of religious intolerance, persecution and war central to this century. Civil wars raged in France, England and Scotland. The horror and devastation of the Thirty Years War (1618–48) in central and northern Europe devastated whole regions. Utopian theorizing of the harmony of nature as a model for educational reform was promoted by Comenius, and his 'internationalism' was aimed at promoting greater understanding and tolerance between the nations through education. This can be understood as a counter to the chaotic irrationality of war and its devastating consequences. These included loss of family, status and national identity. Utopianism also championed the cause of the poor. The question remains as to whether war and the quest for peace and reconciliation are conditions which create reformers. This theme will be explored in relation to all the pioneers in the following chapters.

Like the child, nature also continued to be seen as evil and in need of control. Thomas (1984) argues that by the early modern period the ascendancy of man over nature became an important goal. He goes on to explain how forests and woodlands were still associated with danger and wildness. (To a large degree this is still the case today). In citing Poole's *The English Parnassus* (1657 [1677]), Thomas illustrates the depth of this fear of nature by quoting words from this mid-seventeenth-century poetical dictionary which were used to describe a forest: 'dreadful', 'gloomy', 'wild', 'desert', 'uncouth', 'melancholy', 'unpeopled' and 'beast-haunted' (p. 90). The forest and woods were seen as places where animals, not men, lived. Those who did make squatter dwellings there were seen as outside the law of the land and a source of local conflict with landowners. Thomas adds that even groups of trees by the roadside were seen as potential hiding places for robbers. However, in France, around the year 1600, Thomas notes that nature gradually began to be seen in a new light as a representation of power and a force for good as opposed to evil. The design of the Gardens of Versailles, for example, represented the political power of the monarchy (Mukerjii 1997). Towards the end of the century the beneficence of nature is evident also in the growing interest in nature mysticism among theologians and philosophers who extolled the beauty of mountains. These were features of the landscape which had hitherto been regarded with the same fears attached to woods and forests. This mysticism was to come into its own in the Romantic period where the view was that any improvements to nature were seen as a sign of the destruction of nature. It is this period of turmoil and change which shaped and formed the ideas and influence of Comenius as will be seen in the following section.

The early life and development of Comenius

Comenius was born in 1592 in Nivnice, a small village near the Moravian town of Uhersky Brod. Moravia was a province of what was then the Kingdom of Bohemia. In his biography of Comenius, Panek (1991) tells us that Comenius's father was prosperous, and owned his own house, a farm and fields. He had three sisters. The family were members of a Moravian religious group called *Unitas Fratum* (Unity of Brethren). The Brethren was a dissenting Protestant group descended from the followers of Jan Hus, who was burnt at the stake for heresy in 1415. They condemned class distinctions. As a group they were relentlessly persecuted by Protestants and Catholics alike but managed to survive in the hills of Bohemia and Moravia. This persecution was to be a strong factor in the shaping of Comenius's views.

Death and personal loss were central features in the life of Comenius. His mother and two of his sisters died of the plague when he was just 12 years old and he was sent to live with an aunt in the nearby town of Straznice (Comenius 1998). This was to be the first of many personal losses suffered by Comenius, losses which strongly influenced his later views of children and childhood.

Friends from Straznice sent him to the Latin grammar school at Prerov (Sadler 1970). Here his qualities as a scholar were recognized by his teacher, John Lanecky, and his patron, Charles the Elder of Zerotin, sent him to study at the Calvinist Reformed Gymnasium in Herborn, Germany, an institution which attracted leading scholars of the Continent. Zerotin was a wealthy leader of the Brethren and an influential member of the Upper House of the Bohemian Parliament or Diet (Sadler 1966). This was an important period for the development of educational theories, and many reformed Latin schools and universities at this time were attempting to reform the conditions for learning and studying in the light of an emerging system of educational institutions. At Herborn he came under the influence of his teacher, Johann Heinrich Alsted, who was steeped in the seventeenth-century desire to restore order and control in nature and people's lives amid the chaos of continual war, famine and disease. According to Nordkvelle (2000) he sought to achieve this by writing an encyclopaedia which would encompass all knowledge, while at the same time uniting science, philosophy and theology in this one concept. Alsted was also curious about the 'sciences' of alchemy and astrology, and passed this on to Comenius. This was later to discredit Comenius when his interest in revelations through visions began to influence his work. Comenius later went on to develop this idea with his work on pansophy (which means a system of organizing universal knowledge, here in the form of an encyclopaedia), with a view to completing an encyclopaedia of all phenomena in the world in God's honour. Although the work was never completed, this encyclopaedic approach strongly influenced the content and presentation of his later language books, *Orbis Pictus* in particular, which was originally published in 1658. This book, in Turner's (1972) view, 'represents the entire world in portable form' (p. 113). This was the first ever picture book written for children, using woodcut images from real life.

From Herborn Comenius moved on to begin his theological studies at Heidelberg University and was there from 1613 to 1614. It was then that Comenius was introduced to Bacon's ideas and was encouraged not to specialize but to study everything (Sadler 1970). It was in this wide brief that he began to explore, within his fundamental ecclesiastical framework, a more scientific view of the world. He sought to understand how everything in the universe was connected, sharing with Bacon the view that the accumulation of knowledge was central to human salvation. Here too he began to develop his chiliastic views, believing in the popular doctrine that Christ's return to earth to reign was imminent and that man needed to prepare for this, a coming which would restore harmony to the world. Capkova (1970) argues that Comenius differed from other utopians of his time who envisaged this utopia in extra-European lands or societies. He perceived it in European society itself.

In 1614 he returned to his alma mater in Prerov, Bohemia, where he became a teacher. Here he sought to reform the poor teaching methods by producing a text book for his pupils in order to teach them Latin in a more meaningful way. Sadler (1970) informs us that he also taught them practical skills such as bee keeping. It would be interesting to see how a present-day risk assessment would be worded for such an activity in our current litigious climate. Comenius's focus would undoubtedly have taken risk into consideration but his main focus would have been the lessons to be learnt from the co-operative structure of the beehive community. He loved the countryside and spent many hours exploring. This resulted in him producing the first map of the province of Moravia, which was published in Amsterdam in 1627 (Panek 1991).

After his ordination as a priest in the Brethren in 1616 he was offered a position as a pastor in Fulnek, a predominantly Catholic area just over the border between Moravia and Silesia (Capkova and Frijhoff 1992). Before taking up this post he married Magdalena Vizovsksa, who was from a wealthy family in Prerov, and they had two sons. During his three-year stay in Fulnek, however, he suffered further persecution as the pastor of a minority religious group. Comenius was also known to the authorities as a sympathizer with the revolutionary estates' uprising against the Hapsburg overlords who wanted to keep Bohemia Catholic. The defeat of the estates at the Battle of White Mountain in 1620 made his position in Fulnek untenable. The imperial troops occupied Fulnek and Comenius was forced to go into hiding from 1622 to 1628, sheltered by his former patron, Zerotin. His books became proscribed literature in his own country and were publicly burned in Fulnek in 1623 (Panek 1991). During this period, from 1625 to 1626, Comenius travelled to Poland, Brandenburg and the Netherlands to seek support for the Brethren. He wrote several treatises declaiming against the appalling conditions of the poor, mounting a severe critique of a society which in his view had been led astray by 'an abuse of learning' (Bowen 1981: 83). This criticism took the form of two books, *Labyrinth of the World* and *Paradise of the Heart* (Comenius 1998). Tragically, during this period his wife and two sons died of the plague in his absence.

Comenius remarried in 1624. His new wife, Dorota Cyrillova, was the daughter of Bishop Jan Cyril of the Brethren. In Louthan and Sterk's (1998) translation of *The Labyrinth of the World and the Paradise of the Heart*, Comenius argues that the fate of the Brethren was sealed in July 1627. The Hapsburgs issued a decree proclaiming Catholicism the only official religion of the state. This meant there was no place left for the Czech Brethren in their own country or for other non-Catholics. The Protestant nobility was given a few months to convert or leave the country but the poor had no rights to move so were forced either to convert or leave secretly (Panek 1991). So, Comenius's dreams of peace in his country were dashed and he was forced to uproot once again and go into exile. Under cover of darkness he led a group of believers to join an established group of exiled Brethren in Poland in a small village called Leszno, near the Silesian border. He was never able to return to his homeland.

It was on this journey to Leszno that Comenius developed his interest in revelations when a 17-year-old family companion suffered epileptic fits and made prophecies about the future. Comenius believed that these prophecies came from God. It is important to note here that these older ideas still continued alongside the new, rational, scientific thinking of this early modern period. Mediaeval notions of witchcraft, demon-possession and magic were still a central part of people's lives and Comenius believed in the compatibility between science and Revelation. Panek thought that this belief in religious revelations of a better future made it possible for Comenius to carry on with his work to reform mankind. This extended period of exile from 1628 to 1641 was spent writing and producing some of his finest work such as *Ianua Linguarum Reserata* (The Open Gate of Languages), which was published in Europe and well received. He also completed *Didactica Magna* (The Great Didactic), in which he looked to nature for a new model for educational theory and practice.

Comenius's writing had come to the attention of liberal educational reform groups in England, led by Samuel Hartlib, who published his pansophical manuscripts between the years 1637 and 1639. Comenius reminds us that pansophy was not an entirely new idea but instead a late Renaissance concept which tried to create a new synthesis combining religion, philosophy and science. Hartlib invited Comenius to visit England to help set up a pansophic college. Comenius arrived in 1641 but Civil War broke out soon afterwards and publication was interrupted. Comenius had no choice but to depart from England in 1642 leaving behind for his friends a copy of *Via Lucis* (The Way of Light), which outlined his plan for peace in the world. This work also detailed his plan for a panosophical college which would promote international toler-ance and understanding. Panek argues that this work had a broader intellectual purpose which aimed at educating individuals to liberate their own nations as well as the emancipation of all humanity. His reputation was now well estab-lished in Europe and he was invited to France by Richelieu but declined this offer in favour of an invitation to Sweden from the Dutch–Swedish merchant Laurens de Geer to reform Sweden's educational system. De Geer was to become a very important patron for Comenius. He was a wealthy industrialist who had established Sweden's metallurgical industry and was the principal arms merchant to Gustavus Adolphus, King of Sweden. At that time Sweden was the strongest Protestant power in Europe and sought to consolidate this through educational reform.

Comenius went to stay in Elbing in Prussia from 1642 to 1648 to work on a new set of text books for Swedish schools. Comenius was producing text books for universal education, based on the principles of everyday Latin for practical purposes. The Swedes, however, were looking for advice with teaching classical and literary Latin to their nobility. During this time Comenius worked indefatigably, seeking support from the Swedish government to promote the cause of the Brethren in the hope that they would be able to return to the Czech Lands. The 1648 Treaty of Westphalia did not support their cause, and Comenius and his flock dispersed all over Europe, sadly remaining exiles. (Europe in the seventeenth century looked very different from how it looks today; see Figure 3.2.) Comenius returned to Leszno and was made Bishop in 1632. He was to be the twentieth and last Bishop of the Brethren. In this same year tragedy struck again and his second wife died, leaving him with four chil-dren, the youngest of whom was Daniel, aged 2 years. Comenius (1998) remarks that he soon married again to provide a mother for his children. This time he chose Jana Gajusova, the daughter of a Czech Protestant pastor.

Comenius moved once again, this time to Sarospatak in Transylvania, an independent Hungarian state, where he was offered the chance to try out his pansophic ideas in the Latin school. The experiment was unsuccessful since he found the teachers few and wanting in their attitudes to teaching and to chil-dren. According to Sadler (1966), Comenius concluded that educational reform was useless unless accompanied by social reform. It was here that Comenius, however, wrote his most famous illustrated text book, *Orbis Pictus*, which was later published in 1658. He returned to Leszno in 1654 and remained there until 1656. There was great unrest in Poland at this time. Still in a period of recovery after a war with Russia it had subsequently been invaded again and was now partly occupied by Sweden. In 1656 the Polish army sacked and

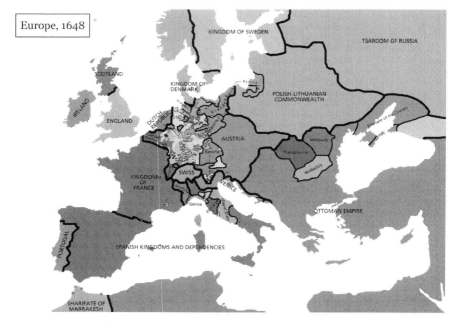

Figure 3.2   Map of Europe in the seventeenth century

burned Leszno and, although he managed to escape, Comenius lost most of his property, including his library and unpublished manuscripts (Panek 1991: 84). Once again he became a destitute fugitive, constantly on the move with his family and fleeing persecution. His old patron Laurens de Geer came to his aid, offering him sanctuary in Amsterdam, where he was to settle for the last 14 years of his life. Since Comenius was well known in the field of European science the city was extremely generous and gave him a small pension and an honorary professorship at the Athenaeum. This was later to become the University of Amsterdam. They also gave him funding to publish his completed works. It was here that *Opera Didactica Omnia* was published in 1658 as well as *Schola Infantiae*, his work on pre-school education.

Comenius did not give up on the cause of the Czech Brethren who were still stranded in Poland after the burning of Leszno. He acquired generous funding for them through his links with the Amsterdam Reformed Church. His passion for peace and reconciliation led him to become involved with the trade wars between England and the Netherlands by attending the Breda Peace Congress in 1667, using it as a platform to present to the assembled diplomats his principles for 'an equitable and just world system' (Panek 1991: 56). Although the Congress did settle the war between England and the Netherlands it was not able to accept Comenius's world plan. He wrote continuously during this period right up until he died in 1670, and urged his son Daniel to assemble his manuscripts for publication. To his death it remained his hope that his lifelong endeavours would lead to a more peaceful, just and humane society.

Implication of his ideas in practice

Comenius was a practical educator and tried to implement his ideas through his teaching. His theory came out of his practice: his observations of children as he worked alongside them informed both his practice and theory. Comenius believed God was the fount of all knowledge and that faith was the only way to access that knowledge. He held that knowledge was essential to human salvation. It was also his view that one could not have a proper understanding of the world without the use of nature and a range of sensory experiences. Knowledge in his view was not innate but derived from these first-hand sensory experiences of the world. He believed that the universe was a harmonious whole, a 'macrocosm' made up of three significant interconnected parts: man, nature and God. Man was a 'microcosm . . . a little world himself and linked to nature' (Capkova 1970: 21). Man and nature were created by God and were therefore imbued with His spirituality. This interconnectedness and interdependence between man and nature, without the spiritual element, is a powerful feature of current Forest School practice and the Swedish *Skogsmulle* and *I Ur och Skur* experiences described in Chapters 7 and 8.

The central theme which underpinned his philosophy was the underlying unity of all human experience as exemplified by nature itself. His thinking became known as 'pansophism'. It was his belief that through observations of nature one could see that the world was whole. He viewed man's classifications as unnatural interventions which destroyed the organic continuity of the real world. This involved seeing the world and knowledge as a whole. 'To achieve knowledge and to reach God . . . in attaining a completely unified view of all existence . . . man fulfils his natural end' (Bowen 1981: 88). These views appealed to educational reformers and statesmen at the time as simple solutions to educational reform. In his great Latin work, *Didactica Magna*, Comenius explained these pansophic views as preaching equality, tolerance, peace and the solidarity of all mankind. To do this he used analogies of harmony and unity in nature. These views were later to be taken up and developed by Rousseau, Pestalozzi and Froebel, all of whom, and Froebel in particular, celebrated nature's animistic qualities.

There is little doubt that Comenius's view of the world was strongly influenced by the views of the religious community of the Brethren. This close-knit organization followed a creed of the democratization of education, something which had been started by Jan Hus and his followers in the fifteenth century. Capkova (1970) informs us that Hus took the view that everyone was made in God's image and therefore had the same right to develop their full potential throughout their lives. (This view included equality for women and 'handicapped children'). Capkova, in discussing the wider sense of the social function of education, believes that Comenius saw this as a very efficient method of social reform.

As part of his great vision Comenius saw education as a lifelong process divided up into different phases or 'schools' as he called them in his *Didactica Magna*. This was later published in Latin, in 1657/58, as part of a four-volume collection of his works *Opera Didactica Omnia* (Assembled Didactical Works). His model for lifelong education can be seen in Table 3.1. The end goal of this programme seems to be concerned with separating out the best students in order to create new leaders of society. It can only be assumed that the less able students stayed with their families and followed their father's chosen occupation. This educational elitism is a feature of Comenius's work, which calls into question our understanding of what exactly he meant by 'universal education'. This would be a subject worthy of further research.

In his writing Comenius attaches great importance to early years education. His approach placed nature at its centre. (It has to be remembered here that 'outdoor learning' as an educational tool for implementing these ideas was not available to Comenius at this time.) His chosen approach can again be attributed to the influence of the Brethren community. Because of repeated persecution in the fifteenth and sixteenth centuries their children were prohibited from attending established schools. A consequence of this was that they developed their own family education programmes (Capkova 1970). The role of the mother in this is very important. The father was regarded as a source of support and security. This ran counter to contemporary thinking where the

Table 3.1 Adapted illustration of Mayer's (1960: 231) view of Comenius's phases of lifelong learning

'School'	Purpose of 'school'
School of mother's knee: birth to 6 years	Child instructed at home with both parents acting as constructive religious and moral models for child
School of vernacular: 6 to 11 years	Child instructed in 'mother tongue' in school plus arts and science
Latin school	More able students instructed in Greek, Latin, Hebrew, science, literature and the arts
University and travel	School for the best students, where leaders of society are created

father was seen as the main educator (see Table 4.1). Comenius's experiences as a child probably influenced this view. His life began with the security of parents and siblings. He would have understood at the age of 12 what it meant to be without that love and security after his parents and siblings died. His experience as a father struggling to bring up a young family after the death of his second wife would also have had a powerful effect on his views. He argued that the early years was the most important stage of development and that teachers needed to be properly trained and highly paid if they were to do their job well. Pugh (2010) raises the same argument today in her bid to improve outcomes for our poorest young children. I would emphasize the urgent need to improve outcomes for all our children by improving training for all teachers and practitioners in their use of the outdoors.

In the 2009 edition of his original book, *The School of Infancy*, Comenius stresses the importance of educating children from as young an age as possible so as to avoid mistakes which would be too difficult to correct later on. Using the metaphor of a tree he argues that '. . . it is impossible to make the tree straight that has grown crooked, or to produce an orchard from a forest everywhere surrounded with briars and thorns' (Comenius 2009: 137). He reinforces this theme in his discussions on discipline. However, he urges caution. This no doubt is based on his own harsh experience and the underlying view that evil lurks beneath the surface. He emphasizes the importance of early intervention: '. . . as soon as weeds, nettles and thistles are discovered, root them out at once, and the crop will come forth so much more abundantly' (p. 164). This view was later echoed in the work of Pestalozzi and Froebel. Using an analogy from nature, Comenius describes children as '. . . celestial plants which need tending and cultivating from the very beginning so that promise enshrined in the seed shall be brought to fruition. In order to prepare for "life wisdom" it is essential to begin early' (Capkova 1970: 18). However, he warns against the danger of separating the child from the mother at too early an age to begin formal education. He believed it was sufficient to learn through play at home. 'The shoot that is taken out when too tender grows feebly and slowly; whereas the firmer one grows strongly and quickly' (Comenius 2009: 170). Pugh (2010) argues the same case with regard to 4-year-olds following a prescriptive curriculum in reception classes today.

Education for young children was seen by Comenius as a preparation for adulthood and for life after death. In *The School of Infancy* he urged parents to ensure that the child's first year should be full of delights, such as singing and being carried around outdoors. He continued, suggesting that the child's second and third years should include time to be in nature with a supportive parent who can help identify and comment on what they see, hear, feel, taste and touch. With this groundwork in place he believed that in their fourth and fifth years children could then begin to differentiate between things, asking for more information with questions such as, What is a stone? What is a horse? and so on.

In advising on good practice, Comenius emphasizes the importance of movement in young children, a central feature of good outdoor learning practice today: '. . . boys may daily meet together . . . play together or run about in open spaces . . . this ought [to be] provided for.' He develops this idea using another metaphor from nature: 'Let them be like ants continually occupied in doing something, carrying, drawing, constructing and transposing, provided always that whatever they do, be done prudently' (2009: 153). This further supports the idea of keeping the child busy to steer him or her away from evil. This notion will also become evident in the chapters on Pestalozzi and Froebel. It is interesting here that although outdoor learning was not a feature of educational practice in the seventeenth century, Comenius exemplifies good practice in the early years by drawing on outdoor examples. The role of the adult in all this, according to Comenius, is to guide and support, never to lead and dominate. This again represents a strong feature of the social structure and organization of the Brethren.

In the *Great Didactic* Comenius outlined nine principles following the order of nature. It was on this that he based his methodology. Table 3.2 shows Mayer's interpretation of this approach. It is clear from this table that Comenius reified nature. Nature to him was self-regulating. It was a thing in its own right which had its own laws. This is very different from how we perceive nature today as something out there to be controlled and regulated by us. Pestalozzi and Froebel's ideas of nature's beneficence were much closer to Comenius's view than ours is today although Frohm and the Forest School approach, for example, without reifying nature emphasize its powerful potential for improving our quality of life.

Throughout his long and turbulent career Comenius tried to put these ideas into practice. In Sarospatak he realized that his method was not enough in itself. Social change needed to happen first. However, it was during his most

Table 3.2 Adapted interpretation of Comenius's methodology in relation to nature's order as outlined in the *Great Didactic* (Mayer 1960: 233)

1	Nature observes a suitable time
2	Nature prepares the material before she begins to give it form
3	Nature chooses a fit subject to act upon, or first submits one to a suitable treatment in order to make it fit
4	Nature is not confused in its operations, but in its forward progress advances distinctly from one point to another
5	In all the operations of nature development is from within
6	Nature, in its formative processes, begins with the universe and ends with the particular
7	Nature makes no leaps, but proceeds step by step
8	If nature commences anything it does not leave off until the operation is complete
9	Nature carefully avoids obstacles and things likely to cause hurt

desperate times as a fugitive and exile that he seemed to be most productive in his writing, his theory and his practice. Frost (1966) argues that his ideas failed to influence educational practice and theory in his own time for a number of reasons. The seventeenth century was not ready to consider the question of universal education. In addition to this he believed in chiliasm and was a member of a religious group which did not accept government authority.

Bowen argues that although Comenius's ideas were not taken up in his own time, they were nonetheless important in the eighteenth century and the work of Locke and then Rousseau was a development of Comenius's ideals. Bowen goes further, suggesting that without the ideas of educational reformers such as Comenius, Hartlib and their supporters, the utopian zeal which drove the Enlightenment forward would not have been so successful. Even though he was committed to Scripture as the source of all authority he nevertheless anticipated the naturalism of Rousseau and Pestalozzi, seeing both as compatible. Each believed in the inherent order in nature and saw this as a model for an organic method. Equally it can be argued that Comenius's sensory, empiricist approach to learning anticipated the nineteenth-century pedagogy of Pestalozzi, who based his method on concrete objects, as did Froebel with his 'gifts' (educational materials designed to meet the child's individual developmental needs) and concepts of kindergarten. Comenius's methodology underpins much of today's approach to early childhood education. It closely resembles many of the principles in the EYFS. It also matches the ethos and philosophy of the Forest School approach to learning, as well as current positive understandings of what outdoor learning is all about.

Reflective questions

Consider the following questions individually or in a group:

- Explain Comenius's belief in education as a social function, including his emphasis on elites.
- Explore the impact of loss on Comenius's views.

4 Born to learn: Johann Heinrich Pestalozzi (1746–1827)

Education and society in the time of Pestalozzi

Figure 4.1   Johann Heinrich Pestalozzi

During the late modern period from 1750 to the present we begin to see the emergence of expertise in the form of education as a nascent 'science'. With this came the appearance of the expert in education, the 'educator'. Pestalozzi was one such 'educator' with particular relevance to the debate on outdoor learning. This is largely with regard to his contribution to the values which underpin good outdoor learning practice today, since the notion of outdoor learning itself was not in use in his time. This contribution will be discussed in greater detail throughout the chapter. However, his ideas were closely bound up with those of other 'educators' such as Robert Owen (1771–1858) and Rousseau. It is therefore important first to consider these 'educators' before moving on to look at Pestalozzi in detail so that we have a clearer understanding of education and society in his time.

Robert Owen, the philanthropist and radical socialist, was one of the early educators who set up an infant school for the children of his factory workers in New Lanark in southern Scotland in 1816. His vision was to change the world by removing children from their parents at as early an age as possible and educating them in an environment which followed a curriculum based on fresh air and exercise. This shift away from parental responsibility for their child's education was of great significance, as was the emphasis on physical health in relation to the outdoor environment. The child appears here as rescued from the evils of poverty and shaped by education in a loving community. What is of interest here is that Owen's ideas did not produce Owenite schools. His ideas were too radical for the time and governments felt threatened by people who challenged the established order at a time of political and social upheaval (Harrison 1969). Perhaps Owen should be viewed as one of the first modern 'educators' since there is little doubt that his emphasis on educational reform for the poor is recognizable in the current Sure Start (DfES 2003d) provision in the UK, as part of a government strategy to reduce child poverty.

The Romantic Movement, and the pedagogy of Rousseau in particular, dramatically changed Western perceptions of childhood. Rousseau's *Emile*, published in 1762, explores how a boy grows up in France, developing naturally from birth under the guidance of a wise teacher. The original innocence of the child is emphasized and the Christian tradition of original sin is banished (Heywood 2001; Valentine 2004). Rousseau, a product of the Enlightenment, shared Owen's fear that adults were potential corrupting influences on the child: 'God makes all things good; man meddles with them and they become evil . . . he will leave nothing as nature intended it' (Rousseau 1780: 5). However, it was not enough to leave it all to nature. It is interesting to note here that although attitudes to children had become secularized, people continued to hold religious beliefs which influenced their thinking (Cunningham 1995). Pestalozzi's Protestantism undoubtedly shaped his pedagogy, as is apparent in the moral code which underpinned his method. At the same time the Puritan influence remained strong and the Evangelical revival movement at the end of the century continued to regard children as 'sinful polluted creatures' (Cunningham 1995: 69). The fact that new ideas emerged does not mean that contradictions between the old and the new disappeared.

During this period we also begin to see the emergence of the child as an individual in his/her own right rather than as an 'imperfect adult', an individual with particular needs which can be met by an informed, attentive adult (Heywood 2001: 23). In *Emile* Rousseau urged mothers to become involved again in the business of childrearing. (He was of the opinion that if fathers had been intended by nature for this role they would have been born with breasts.) The seventeenth-century view of the father having sole responsibility for the education and development of his children was coming to a close.

A strong feature of Romanticism was the notion that childhood was important and should be a happy time. Indeed it is at this time that the idea of happiness as a goal of human design emerged. The hope was that if those qualities of childhood could be preserved into adulthood then there was hope for the redemption of the adult world (Cunningham 1995). This was a reflection of Owen's aims for his school in New Lanark. This belief in the original innocence and purity of the child and the adult as protector was also reflected in the works of poets such as Coleridge and Wordsworth (Wyness 2006). It was in 1800 that the 'wild boy of Aveyron' (Victor) was found in the woods in France. Jean Marc Gaspard Itard (1751–1838), the French physician renowned for his work with deaf-mutes at this time, worked to rehabilitate him. This fuelled a contemporary debate on environments for learning. The issue of nature–nurture came into play and, in this particular case, the advisability of taking the wildness of nature out of the boy (Spodek 1988). Itard's pupil, Edouard Seguin (1812–80), was later to strongly influence the work of Margaret McMillan.

The awareness of beauty in nature which emerged in the Italian Renaissance continued to grow and became integral to the philosophy behind the Landscape Movement. The dual role of nature and art came together in the design of the garden. From the 1820s onwards, advocates such as John Claudius Loudon (1783–1843), a Scottish botanist, and garden and cemetery designer, were agitating for public parks to be accessible to all as essential breathing spaces for city workers (Hobhouse 2002). In Table 4.1 I have developed a framework which illustrates these far-reaching changes in ideas with regard to children, parenthood, childhood and nature during this 1500–1900 period.

Following a period of revolution and counter-revolution in Europe, Romantic ideas were put to one side. The political power of the developing modern state in the nineteenth century had as its main focus the creation of social order by consolidating territorial power. This was in the contemporary context of very rapid economic and social change. Robert Owen was the first of many trying to cope with these changes. Much of this change was exemplified in the development and influence of Pestalozzi himself.

Table 4.1   Changing ideas of children, parenthood, childhood and nature from 1500 to 1900

Period	Perception of children	Perception of parenthood	Perception of childhood	Perception of nature
Mediaeval Britain 1100–1500 Mediaeval Europe 500–1500	Children were viewed as miniature adults	The mother had a primary caring role. Parents prepared the child for adult world of work	The idea of childhood as we perceive it now did not exist	Nature was perceived as wild and dangerous
The modern period: early modern 1500–1750	Children were regarded as evil	The father took a leading role in the care and education in the family	Childhood began to be defined in opposition to adulthood	Nature represented order and beauty, and began to become a space to enjoy
The modern period: late modern 1750 to present	Young children are seen as innocent and in need of rescue and protection. Older children are considered to be out of control, a danger to society and the focus of legislation	Parents are perceived as working in partnership with the state to nurture and educate children. However, the state intervenes more and more as to *how* to raise children	Childhood is considered as a right for every child and as separate from adulthood	Nature becomes romanticized as a model for life

The early life and development of Pestalozzi

Johann Heinrich Pestalozzi was born in Zurich in 1746, the second of three children, into the privileged section of Zurich society. He came from a family which emigrated from Italy in the sixteenth century. His mother's family was well connected and included a number of well-known physicians. His father, a surgeon and oculist, died when he was 6 years old, leaving the family with reduced means. He was brought up by his mother and a servant called Babeli, who swore faithful, lifelong allegiance to the family. Pestalozzi was greatly influenced by his grandfather, a rural pastor who ran a small village school for the poor. Silber quotes Pestalozzi saying that here he discovered that 'The ragged village children had lived carefree and healthy lives until the age of 5 or 6 when the double misery of the ABC one-sidedness and the cotton industry smothered their vitality' (Silber 1973: 7). His observations of the poor, simple lives of the villagers inspired him to begin a lifelong career concerned with social justice, taking an active interest in country life and country people from his early youth.

Pestalozzi was educated in Zurich at the elementary abbey school. He moved on to the grammar school, the Collegium Humanitatis, and then to the Collegium Carolinum where he studied philology and philosophy. Here he came under the influence of progressive, political thinkers. Zurich was famous at this time as a centre of radical thought and was also the literary capital of the German-speaking world. Pestalozzi became angered by the politically unjust nature of the centralized city-state, which was a 'democracy' in name only. It was, in reality, a patriciate. Citizenship was unattainable for the majority since it was handed down from father to son among the higher classes. As a way of preserving its self-interest in the city-state the oligarchic government repressed democratic practice and equality of rights. Silber explains how country people outside the city had limited rights and were excluded from all spheres of public life. Reacting against this inequality, Pestalozzi joined a radical group called the 'Patriots'. This was a youth movement concerned with raising the country's moral standards: 'Inspired by Rousseau and the moral precepts of the Enlightenment . . . they had a strict sense of duty, practised self-denial and restraint and put claims of the country before personal desires' (Silber 1973: 8–9). They produced a newsletter called the *Moral Weekly* and became involved in politics uncovering abuses of power, including cases of government embezzlement. Pestalozzi left the Collegium without completing his degree and did not proceed, as expected, into law or the church, but chose agriculture instead.

At this time, a key shift in thinking occurred where the Romantic vision of nature took on religious significance (Bowen 1981). There was an overall awareness of a grand creator, and nature itself became imbued with spirituality. This pantheist notion that God is everything and everything is God strongly influenced Pestalozzi, and Froebel even more so. Such views strongly challenged contemporary orthodoxy. Silber notes that critics of Pestalozzi's method claimed that it was atheistic and 'not properly Christian' (1973). What is interesting here, however, is that while these new ideas clashed with orthodox views, a new accord was reached with religion in which pantheism questioned contemporary notions of sin and the evil child.

The idealization of women during this period as the natural carers for young children in the home also informed Pestalozzi's view that mankind cannot begin to understand God if 'he' has not first experienced the love of a mother as well as a father in a family. In this view the mother indeed was the dominant influence, with the father playing only a supporting role, a view Pestalozzi shared with Comenius. He believed that the road to religion and the knowledge of God lay in the path of observing and imitating good behaviour within the family. He saw the mother as 'the mediator between the child and nature' and a 'higher being', a position which distinguished her from the animals (Silber 1973: 175). According to Pestalozzi, the mother was 'God's representative on earth' [who] 'leads the child to truth and through his association of her loved person with his environment, to universal love' (Silber 1973: 175). The spheres of influence in a child's life as understood by Pestalozzi are illustrated in Figure 4.2 (adapted from Silber 1973: 178).

Romanticism also understood education to be essential in promoting a new, enlightened society. Bowen argues that *Emile* should be seen as proceeding from Enlightenment thinking and utopian theorizing. The tradition of religious utopianism is a much older one of which Comenius was representative. Pestalozzi's own educational experiences as a child and youth also greatly influenced his method. He was appalled, as was Comenius before him, by his experiences of his own teachers, describing them as untrained people who hated their role. In his most famous work, *How Gertrude Teaches Her Children* (Pestalozzi

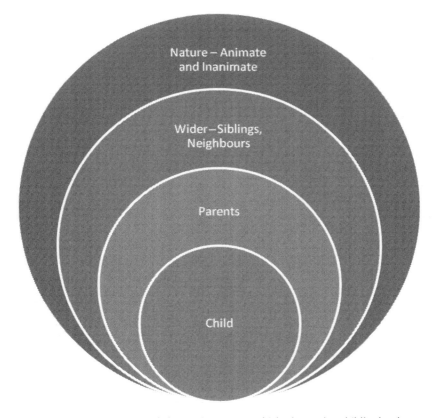

Figure 4.2 Pestalozzi's view of the environments which shape the child's development (adapted from Silber 1973: 178)

1907), Pestalozzi, like Comenius before him, portrayed children and childhood as symbols of innocence and simplicity, analogous to the same qualities in the external world of nature. Like Comenius, Pestalozzi draws on the holism of nature as an example for educational reform. The child was compared with a seed which needed to be nurtured in a loving environment; a seed which contained the essence of intellect and personality. Now seen as separate from adults and requiring different treatment the child was beginning to be seen as an 'individual'. Childhood was still, nonetheless, regarded by Pestalozzi as a preparation for adulthood, in the vocational sense of a trade being useful for future survival. His philosophy was, like Owen's, that these children would never develop into useful citizens if they were not guided by adults. Unlike Owen, however, Pestalozzi felt this could take place within the supportive structure of the family, a view strongly taken up by McMillan in the twentieth century.

Pestalozzi maintained that the key to a successful life was love, work and interaction with others. He strongly acknowledges, however, that his own upbringing in an intensely protective atmosphere, where he was not allowed to play with other children, lacked this balance:

> He was not allowed to play with them in the street; so he did not know their games, their ways, their secrets . . . When he met them by chance he behaved awkwardly and was laughed at by them all. When he was about nine or ten they nicknamed him 'Harry Queer of Foolstown'.
>
> (Silber 1973: 5)

Despite the devotion of his mother and Babeli he felt he was not equipped socially in his early childhood with the skills needed for later life. Silber adds that the absence of a father to guide him and teach him a trade further compounded his sense of inadequacy. These experiences strongly influenced his approach to learning, especially his belief that education by itself was not enough. Without practical training and the ability to socialize with others it was worthless. The influence of women in his upbringing was undoubtedly to play a large part in the exalted position he gave 'the mother' in his educational philosophy. This differs from Comenius's emphasis on the importance of the mother, which was based on personal experiences of the absence of a mother in childhood through death. Pestalozzi's views regarding the role of the father as a strong supporting influence within the family are best described in his experiences at Stans, where he became mother and father to the children he cared for.

The influence of the Enlightenment also led him to '. . . a new interest in country life and new theories of agriculture and economics. The school of the Physiocrats [advocates of government by a scientific notion of natural order] now saw the wealth of the nation in its soil, not, as the Mercantilists, in its trade' (Silber 1973: 3). Societies for the study of nature were founded all over Europe, reflecting the growth of Physiocracy. *Emile* appeared at this time, attacking the present state of society and calling people back to nature. The mediaeval view of man as 'outside nature' was opposed by Rousseau's view of a holistic world. Pestalozzi, a young student with radical views, was strongly influenced by this book. He acknowledged his debt to Rousseau, even to the extent of naming his son Jean-Jacques and rearing him according to the principles expressed in Rousseau's writing.

Following Rousseau's call, Pestalozzi went back to nature when he turned to agriculture on leaving the Collegium, a radical step down for a man of his social class. The call of the natural life appealed greatly to him and he hoped to be able to work for the poor. He served his apprenticeship on a farm in Birr, which was in Aargau. This was one of the most northern cantons of Switzerland. He worked for Tschifelli, an agrarian pioneer, who was engaged in experimenting with increasing the productivity of the land in order to improve the well-being of the population as a whole (Heafford 1967). Tschifelli, a gentleman farmer with a private income, was familiar with the theory of agriculture as well as being a member of Berne Economic Society. This connection between cultivating the land and cultivating the people was part of that aspect of the Enlightenment concerned with the reform of civil society. Planning to follow Tschifelli's methods, Pestalozzi acquired a piece of moorland and there established a farm of his own. He later transformed the farmhouse into a school, calling it Neuhof (New Farm), and continued to practise these same innovative agricultural ideas alongside, and as part of, his teaching, in which gardening became a central feature. It was this use of the outdoors to promote learning which Froebel later adopted and developed. Interestingly, gardening has become central to good outdoor practice in schools today. It is also promoted by the Allotment Society. Groups such as Incredible Edibles encourage the growing of fruit and vegetable in disused public spaces to encourage healthy growing and eating in our current economic recession. However, Pestalozzi's project at Neuhof was not sustainable financially and he had to close the school. He suffered substantial financial loss and sold off some of the land, subsequently losing the respect of his previous sponsors (Heafford 1967).

In 1769 he married Anna Schultless, a mature woman from an aristocratic background whose family was opposed to the union because of Pestalozzi's lack of income. They had one son. Pestalozzi turned to writing to make a living. He concentrated on developing his method and kept his interest in educational reform alive by writing short moral tales. He went on to set up a school at Stans, an institute at Burgdorf and another in Yverdun. He died at Neuhof in 1827, aged 81.

He shared with Rousseau the view that the psychology of the child is significantly different from that of adults and should be valued in its own right (Postman 1994). The foundations of all their work emphasized the belief that education must work in harmony with the child's nature as well as with the laws of nature itself (Abbott and Gillen 2000). Pestalozzi moved about between these different concepts in his writing, often resulting in a lack of clarity. A major criticism of him, in fact, is that he never fully clarified and documented his own educational methods. Silber sums up his position regarding nature in the following way: 'These laws are the same for external nature and human nature, for man was created in accordance with nature and his powers and faculties are, within limits, in conformity with the forces of nature' (1973: 136). Pestalozzi had tremendous faith in this position, believing that since nature is one there can only be one method of education. This method, he asserted, should be in accordance with universal nature. His biggest claim was that this approach will 'lead man back to his own better nature and will bring out his full humanity' (Silber 1973: 136). Pestalozzi is arguing here against his own observations of contemporary educational practice, which he felt appealed to man's baser nature and was responsible for the barbaric conditions in which people lived. In following the laws of nature man will get back to the state of innocence with which he was born, a view he shared with Comenius.

This Romantic view of nature was by far the largest factor in Pestalozzi's inheritance and the biggest contributor to our present interest in outdoor learning. Nature, he came to realize, was the means by which he could deliver his message. In *How Gertrude Teaches Her Children* he uses powerful imagery from nature itself to describe this journey from despair to hope:

> I saw popular instruction like a bottomless swamp before my eyes; and waded round and round, with difficulty, in its mire, until at last I learned to know the sources of its waters, the causes of its obstructions, and the places from which there might be a possibility of diverting its foul waters.
>
> (Pestalozzi 1907: 9)

Implication of his ideas in practice

There was a move away from voluntary organizations towards more state responsibility at this time (Cunningham 1995). Postman (1994: 56) argues that the state began to intervene as protectors of children, in a partnership between parents and government which was designed to take responsibility for children's nurturing. The absolutist states of Prussia and France were already trying to develop mass education in the 1770s and 1780s but were interrupted by revolution and war (Cunningham 2006). It is only in the nineteenth century that the needs of the state become more marked. With economic advances in democratic and liberal states, it became imperative that the enfranchised poor should be educated and that the state should fully institute the schemes that had failed to develop earlier. By the 1860s the state had the means and the determination to do this. As Disraeli famously remarked in the debate preceding the Reform Act of 1867, 'We have to educate our masters' (Hansard 1884).

In order to understand and illustrate Pestalozzi's influence it is necessary now to look at his practice. This will be considered in the light of the schools and institutes where he worked. These were in Neuhof, Stans and Burgdorf, all near Berne, and Yverdun, a French-speaking town at the southern end of Lake Neuchatel (Bowen 1981).

Neuhof 1774–79

Pestalozzi moved from his failed ambition to grow crops on his farm at Neuhof in Birr to 'growing children', nurturing the seeds which contained their intellect and personality. Bowen notes that he was concerned about the economic inadequacy of the poor and became aware that they needed a vocational education if they were to become economically independent and achieve their potential as human beings. In a time when popular education was in everybody's minds it is significant that Pestalozzi took this radical position on vocational education. He took in 'state-ward orphans' who worked for their keep, offering them in return a basic education in arithmetic and the catechism (Bowen 1981: 220). In the evening, by way of recreation, the boys would do gardening and the girls cooking and sewing. Pestalozzi depended on humanitarians and benefactors to support his venture. Unfortunately, little was forthcoming so he had to close the school.

Pestalozzi continued to live at Neuhof for twenty years. Silber (1973: 42) claims that what moved him away from his prioritizing 'paternal influence' in *The Evening Hour of a Hermit* to the mother in *Leonard and Gertrude* was his wife's enduring qualities during this period of destitution. The family often lacked the bare essentials and rarely went into town or to church because their clothes were so worn. He became the laughing stock of the people, the local populace calling him 'Pestilence' or 'Scarecrow' (Silber 1973: 26). These were sad echoes of the teasing and name calling he endured as a child. Like Comenius before him, it is remarkable that during this desolate period of poverty he did not give up but continued writing and developing his theories. In 1798 he was rescued by the offer of an editorship of a Swiss newspaper. After this he accepted the offer of a school at Stans.

Stans 1798

The period leading up to the French Revolution was receptive to new educational theories and Pestalozzi was hopeful that his ideas would be widely adopted. He was well connected and had access to government officials and even monarchs. As part of his campaign to reform society through education he became an early version of what was later to become 'the educational lobbyist'. He sought support at the highest levels in France, Prussia and Switzerland. He was willing to travel widely to promote his ideals,

Figure 4.3   Detail from the 1879 oil on canvas painting 'Pestalozzi with the orphans in de: Stans' by Konrad Grob (1828–1904)

understanding well the importance of the state in promoting educational reform (Heafford 1967). The French state at this time was greatly interested in the possibilities of popular education, and favoured his ideas so much that they made him a citizen of France. However, the political unrest following the revolutionary period of the eighteenth century put paid to his aspirations, and confidence in his unorthodox methods declined.

The French moved into Switzerland in 1799, taking over the Swiss Confederacy and replacing it with a new federal government. Out of this political instability came the opportunity to set up another school in Stans, a small town which had been ravaged by the invading French moving south to Italy. Appalled by the atrocity, the French government set up a school for the town's children and invited Pestalozzi to be the head. Pestalozzi faced many difficulties at Stans, not least of which was the fact that he was seen by the parents as an emissary of the hated French government. Despite this, Pestalozzi describes his work at Stans as the happiest days of his life. Here, even though he was working in a government institution, he only employed one other person to help him in the education of the school's seventy children. He used only natural teaching aids such as nature itself alongside the children's regular routines and self-initiated activities inside and outside. This approach to learning is clearly illustrated today in the UK Forest Schools. It was in this school that he proved his theory to himself, especially 'that the characteristics of a home had to be emulated in institutional upbringing, that the spirit of the living room was the basis of good education, and that parental love was the first demand of a good educator' (Silber 1973: 113, citing Pestalozzi). He became everything to the child. He spent many of the following years trying to find a monarch who could fill a similar patriarchal role.

Burgdorf 1800–04

Pestalozzi was offered an alternative appointment at Burgdorf. Here he established an institute which flourished for five years. It was there he realized his ambition to teach the poor alongside his fee-paying boys. His ideas matured rapidly and were published in 1801 as *How Gertrude Teaches Her Children* (Bowen 1981). Pestalozzi established his methods with the support of the Society of the Patriotic Friends of Education. This Society is a further example of the proliferation of civil society reform groups who were active at this time. This group was promoting ideas about education and favoured his approach as part of their plan to set up a national teacher's training college for the new Swiss Republic (Bowen 1981). The school became well known and Pestalozzi's theories became very popular. Many followers of his method came to work with him at Burgdorf.

However, in 1802 Napoleon revised the Swiss constitution, dissolving the central government and giving all power back to the cantons. Burgdorf came under the administration of the Berne canton, which was not sympathetic to his ideas and withdrew its support (Heafford 1967). Pestalozzi was challenged, not for his unorthodox methods but for his idea of religion. He and his friends believed that his religious ideas were 'truly Christian' (Silber 1973: 159). His severest critics were conservative groups connected to orthodox branches of Calvinism. The outcome of this was a statement from the Berne council stating that Pestalozzi's institute at Burgdorf 'lacked proper Christian instruction' and therefore had to close' (pp. 15–18). The withdrawal of government financial support for the school forced Pestalozzi to think again. He went into partnership with Philipp Emmanuel von Fellenberg (1771–1844), another educational pioneer, who ran an experimental farm and institute which focused on practical and vocational education modelled on Pestalozzi's *Leonard and Gertrude* (Frost 1966). Pestalozzi hoped that Fellenberg's good business sense, a quality Pestalozzi did not feel he himself possessed, would complement his educational work. The project failed, however, and Pestalozzi moved to Yverdun.

Yverdun 1805–25

This period is often seen as Pestalozzi's most productive. The school was originally set up for fee-paying boys but was later open to girls. There was a free option for the poor. Yverdun became an important centre for education. Pestalozzi refined his methods there and attracted worldwide attention. As time went on he became more and more involved in his research and spent less time teaching, a possible explanation for the eventual collapse of relationships within the Institute. He was interested in the careful observation of children and worked at a practical level with them. His method had two parts:

1 General method: the main focus of this part was to create a secure and loving environment where the child's self-esteem and confidence were fostered and were of central importance for future learning. This remains a fundamental element which underpins good outdoor learning practice today.
2 Special method: this part focused on learning based on the child's experience. In addition, continuity, for example between different stages of learning and the stages of transition between home and school, was important here, as it had been with Comenius (Gutek 1972: 210).

Pestalozzi's 'object lesson' was central to this. He believed that education should begin with concrete, natural objects which the child could fully explore at his/her leisure. This he saw as a prerequisite for concept development and the labelling of objects. The secret of his method, according to Gutek, was to present the right object at the right time, allowing the child to work and play with it and in so doing build its own concepts of its nature, before being guided by the adult to explore wider descriptions and properties of the object. This notion was to be explored in depth by Froebel, as will be seen in the next chapter. Mayer clearly illustrates Pestalozzi's vision of the role of the adult in the child's learning. He cites a diary entry of Pestalozzi:

> Lead your child out into nature, teach him on the hilltops and in the valleys. Then he will listen better and the sense of freedom will give him more strength to overcome difficulties . . . let him be taught by Nature, rather than by you . . . should a bird sing or an insect hum on a leaf, at once stop your walk; bird and insect are teaching him; you may be silent.
>
> (Mayer 1960: 286)

While outdoor learning was not a known concept of his time, Pestalozzi, like Comenius, used examples of outdoor activities in nature to illustrate good practice, believing that the external world of nature was an excellent model for educational and societal reform.

After the Revolution many people came from all over the world to observe and learn from his practice in Yverdun. Sir James Phillips Kay-Shuttleworth (1804–77), an English politician, educationalist and founder of training colleges for teachers, came to observe these methods as a possible base for mass education in Britain. Because of its collapse after the Napoleonic wars Prussia sent many young men to train as teachers with a view to restoring their ravaged country through educational reform. At this time Pestalozzi wrote 34 letters to James Pierrepoint Greaves, an English admirer who had worked with him at Yverdun from 1818 to 1822, in order to learn the theory of the method with a view to applying it in England. It is in these letters that Bowen claims Pestalozzi sets down the clearest description of his educational theory and practice. The letters were translated into English in 1827 in a volume called *Letters on Early Education* and so the Pestalozzi method spread to the English-speaking world.

At the end of his time at Yverdun, when the institute was near closure, Pestalozzi published his complete works as a potential source of funding to keep the institute open. Subscribers to this were the Czar of Russia and the kings of Prussia and Bavaria. That he could call on such figures illustrates his considerable fame and influence at the time. Sadly, the money came too late to save his venture. He left Yverdun in 1825 aged 79, after many crises and disagreements with the staff, and returned to Neuhof to concentrate on his writing (Heafford 1967). He died in Neuhof in 1827.

Pestalozzi's ideas were taken up in some Protestant parts of Northern Europe, promoted often by enthusiasts such as Greaves (Silber 1973). Although this pedagogy travelled to England, Silber argues that it arrived both 'too early' and 'too late' to be accepted. It was 'too early' in the sense that interest in popular education at that time had just begun and was still bound up in religious education. 'Too late' in so far as Pestalozzi was an old man by the time his ideas reached England (Silber 1973: 304). By this time his institute at Yverdun had lost its reputation. Silber goes on to suggest that his approach was not taken up by Catholic countries in Europe since it was considered irreligious. He achieved some success in establishing his pedagogy in America but again its ultimate decline was a result of being introduced too early (p. 314).

Pestalozzi's legacy

Pestalozzi's legacy, like that of Comenius, can be seen in the essential values which support good outdoor practice today. Outdoor learning was not a feature of contemporary practice. However, his view of children as individuals with particular needs is central to EYFS educational theory and practice today and to outdoor learning in particular. The concomitant strategies for providing for those individual needs started with Comenius and were then developed by Pestalozzi. His close observations of children enabled him to design an environment, inside and outside, to suit their needs. Observation continues to be a central feature of good practice today. His method established that a secure environment was essential for future learning. This is one of the most important principles of good outdoor practice today.

Despite, or, it could be argued, *because* of personal loss, persecution and the impact of war, Pestalozzi, like Comenius before him, persevered with his passion to reform society through education, beginning with the youngest children. While Pestalozzi was at Yverdun, Owen came to visit him, as did Froebel. It was the element of nature in Pestalozzi's philosophy, linking childhood and the outdoors, which Froebel took up, using the garden as the natural interface between the child and nature itself. In the following chapter an exploration of the influences which impacted on Froebel as he tried to execute these ideas will be followed by a consideration of their influence on the present.

Reflective questions

Consider the following questions individually or in a group:

- What were the main factors which shaped Pestalozzi?
- What impact did war have on Pestalozzi's views?

---

5 Born to do: Friedrich Froebel (1782–1852)

Education and society in the time of Froebel

Figure 5.1 Friedrich Froebel

Froebel contributed significantly to emergent notions of education as a 'science'. He made two visits to Pestalozzi in Yverdun, the second lasting two years. On both occasions he returned full of admiration for Pestalozzi but critical of what he referred to as a lack of 'organic connection' between the subjects taught. He saw Pestalozzi's method as 'too empirical' and 'not scientific enough' (Bowen 1981: 336). Led by his own educational background in natural science and crystallography at the Universities of Jena and Berlin, he turned for inspiration to Joseph Priestley (1733–1804), whose religious Enlightenment theory of holistic science and *Naturphilosophie* was trying to 'create an organic view of nature and man's relationship to it' (Bowen 1981: 331). Priestley, a dissenting clergyman, theologian and political theorist, is often credited with the discovery of oxygen, but he took an especial interest in considering how science could improve the quality of human life. In the light of Priestley's view Froebel codified Rousseau and Pestalozzi's ideas into a scientific system in keeping also with Alexander von Humboldt's (1769–1859) view of 'man, nature and knowledge as a dynamically interrelated whole' (Bowen 1981: 332). Humboldt, a German naturalist and explorer, is regarded as one of the founders of modern geography and as one of Europe's great scientists. This promotion of education as a science in the late eighteenth and early nineteenth century continued to be resisted by established religion since it was felt that it had no basis in faith and threatened the religious–classical tradition in the West. While Pestalozzi and Froebel shared the Romantic view that the organic world came from God, contemporaries such as Humboldt and Charles Darwin (1809–82), for example, were careful not to associate with these divine links, so as to avoid any religious controversy. As the century progressed and science became more closely linked with industrialization and material wealth the concept of education as a science became more acceptable and widely used.

Froebel was not the only person thinking about unity and connectedness at this time. His views can be seen against the contemporary background of philosophical debate concerning unity. For example, in 1818, the same year that Froebel set up his first infant school in Keilhau, 'Musicians, poets and philosophers were . . . demonstrating how things belonged together and so too were the scientists . . . a close analysis of oxygen, hydrogen, carbonic acid and nitrogen was leading to the organic theory' (Bowen 1981: 9).

From his close observations of children at play, Froebel developed Pestalozzi's ideas on child development and provided a theoretical basis for early childhood education which recognized not just stages of physical growth but stages of intellectual growth as well. Froebel took his liberal, humanist ideas on child development a stage further and drew attention to the 'preschool' child whose needs, he felt, were not always met at home and yet were not able to be met at school either. In order to meet these needs he created a space in which children could develop. In fact, development was equated directly with physical growth, Froebel later calling this space a *kindergarten*, a garden of, and for, growing children.

Although he valued highly the Romantic view of the mother and family as the child's first educators, he believed that young children also benefited socially from being exposed to a wider community which included nature. These Romantic notions of an organic community fitted well with his own leanings towards botany and the natural sciences. Like Owen and Pestalozzi, he believed that the quality of the environment where this experience of community took place was of central importance. 'Quality' remains a strong feature of current early years provision although its focus is largely concerned with auditing practice. Contemporary developmental thinkers also held this view that the broader environment mattered and it was felt that children needed an environment where they themselves could initiate learning appropriate to their biological stages of development. This view strongly reflects the first stage in Pestalozzi's method where the establishment of a secure environment is seen as a necessary prerequisite to learning. It is also strongly reflected in good outdoor practice today.

At Blankenburg, in 1837, where he had his first experience of working with 'pre-school' children, Froebel developed a learning programme. He wrote, 'Growing plants are cultivated in accordance with Nature's laws, so here in our child garden, our kindergarten, shall be the noblest of all growing things' (Fuller 2007: 35). This approach to learning was a reaction against the growth in scientific, specialist expertise as the century progressed, a growth emphasizing learning as a receptive process which, in Froebel's view, did not take into account the child's need to be active. It is this essential element of 'learning by doing' which Froebel added to Pestalozzi's method of learning through the senses. This element continues to feature in current outdoor practice.

Immanuel Kant (1724–1804) and Johann Gottlieb Fichte (1762–1814) inspired German educators like Froebel to turn their attention to what educators feel to be the unity and interdependent forces of the natural world (Fuller 2007: 37). From this position Froebel came to argue for structure in children's lives in order to lead them to an understanding and appreciation of the organic world. Play, as part of that structure, had to be taken seriously as 'a child's work', and learning materials should be presented at the moment when their innate developmental interest was ready to receive them. These materials took the form of 'gifts' and 'occupations' in Froebel's system. This is a key shift from Pestalozzi's approach which included only materials naturally found in the child's environment.

The 'gifts' were didactic toys designed to increase dexterity and teach the unity of the laws of nature. In France at this time, inspired by Jean Marc Gaspard Itard (1774–1838), an educator of deaf-mutes including the wild boy of Aveyron, Edouard Seguin (1812–80) was developing teaching materials of a similar didactic, scientific nature to teach children with mental disabilities. Montessori in Italy was later to adopt these ideas and create auto-didactic teaching aids which, incidentally, she refused to attribute in any way to Froebel's ideas (Lawrence 1952). Through the 'occupations' of clay, sand, weaving and paper folding, for example, children were to be taught how to be good citizens and understand the role their labour played in the good of the community. Gardening was a particularly good example of this. Each child had his or her own plot of land to look after and produce goods of benefit to the community. Froebel saw the work they did there to be of great educational importance, developing children intellectually as well as physically and socially. Pestalozzi, on the other hand, saw such activities as a preparation for the inevitable duties of adulthood. Both 'gifts' and 'occupations' were offered in the context of play. The children spent a lot of time outside discovering how materials and shapes helped to form the natural world. In this way they would be led to see how the materials they handled were part of a holistic universe.

The early life and development of Froebel

In her book commissioned by the governing body of the Froebel Society to celebrate the centenary of Froebel's death, Lawrence (1952) explains that Froebel's childhood was a lonely one. His mother died when he was just nine months old and although his new stepmother was kind to him initially she quickly lost interest when she gave birth to her own child. Born in 1782 in Oberweissbach, in the Thuringian area of Prussia, which is now part of Germany, he was the fifth son of the village pastor. White (1909) notes that his father let him help around the house and in the garden. His father believed he would receive a better education at a girls' school rather than at the local mixed village school. This exposure would, no doubt, have further contributed to his loneliness and have influenced his later views of education as a sociable and co-operative activity. At the age of 10 he was rescued by a maternal uncle, another pastor, who gave him love and a more normal schooling. His uncle also allowed him the freedom to roam at will in the mountains of his home locality. This is how he began to nurture his love of plants and nature.

He tried his hand at various occupations, first, in 1797, as an apprentice to a forester where he did little forestry but had, according to White, unlimited access to the forester's library of books about nature. He subsequently worked as a steward on a farm and later went to Jena University where one of his brothers was studying medicine. Lawrence notes that during this time he fell into debt and, because his father refused to help, spent nine weeks in prison. His father eventually repaid the debt, but only on condition that he renounced all claims to a family inheritance. Fortunately, he was left a small inheritance by the uncle who rescued him from his stepmother and thus, in 1805, he went to Frankfurt to study architecture. It was there that he met Anton Gruner, a former pupil of Pestalozzi who ran what was regarded then as a progressive school. He persuaded Froebel to take up a teaching post there and to visit Pestalozzi's school in Yverdun in Switzerland. Froebel, though impressed with what he saw, was also critical of staff discipline and the lack of coherence in Pestalozzi's methods, as well as his unwillingness to theorize his method. Pestalozzi felt it was unnecessary to do anything other than simply allow his method to be expressed in practice. Froebel later returned to Yverdun where, in 1808, he became a tutor to three boys. He insisted to their parents that the children should leave home and live and work solely with him in the country-side outside Yverdun. There they would focus mainly on nature study and gardening. Owen comes to mind here, believing, as Froebel did, that children need to be removed from parents if their education was to be effective. Such a demand today in our present culture of parental choice and child protection would be unthinkable.

In 1811 he returned to Germany, to Göttingen University, and studied the natural sciences, which he felt were essential tools for an educator. A year later he went to Berlin University where he studied crystallography, miner-alogy and natural history under Professor Weiss, the originator of the science of crystallography. His studies were interrupted when he joined the army. In the aftermath of the Prussian defeat of Jena by Napoleon in 1806 many students became politicized, developing a consciousness of the brotherhood of all Germans, beyond Prussia alone. Germany was not yet a state at this time. Prussia was part of the Holy Roman Empire of the German nation.

Froebel seems to have enlisted out of a sense of this growing nationalism. In 1813 he joined the nationalist Lutzow Free Corps in Leipzig, which consisted in large part of student and academic volunteers from all over Germany. Froebel saw active service, engaging in battle as a rifleman and serving until Napoleon was defeated and the First Peace of Paris in 1814. This experience undoubtedly fired his enthusiasm for German nationhood, as well as increasing his awareness of the importance of education in producing social change. The powerful impact of war made the same impression on Comenius and Pestalozzi, both of whom believed that a better world could follow the destruction of war. War also clearly inspired Froebel and Comenius's work on the vernacular as a means of promoting a sense of identity as a nation. Froebel's war experience also increased his desire to discover unity in the world. These ideas came to fruition after the war when he took a position as curator of the mineralogical museum in Berlin under Weiss. Through his daily observations of the natural forms and properties of the minerals and crystals in his care he came to an understanding of how he could create unity in an educational philosophy which would unite the home, the school and the world.

Froebel met Wilhelm Middendorff and Heinrich Langethal while in the Free Corps. They helped him set up a school in Griesham after he left the museum. The school moved to Keilhau in 1818, the same year that Froebel married. The Keilhau School became well known as a place where character training and a love of nature, including work on the land, were instilled. This was quite different from the traditional 'curriculum' of reading and the clas-sics. Froebel put his practice into writing and published *The Education of Man* in 1826. The school came under scrutiny by the authorities for being too revolutionary, and parents began to withdraw their children. This caused a severe financial crisis for Froebel and he was forced to close the school. He left Germany in 1831 and tried to set up two schools in a Catholic canton in Switzerland. His views were not accepted there either and he was branded a heretic by the Jesuits and forced to move on yet again (Weston 2000). Again, this theme of persecution and its consequences is evident, presenting a strong link with both Comenius's and Pestalozzi's experience.

He moved to Burgdorf, in Switzerland, in 1831, where he took up the position of head of an orphanage, one which in fact had previously been run by Pestalozzi. Again emphasizing the specific needs of young children, he developed a series of graduated exercises suited to the age and interest of the child. This approach, practised also by Comenius and Pestalozzi, is strongly evident today in the 'start from where the child is' approach advocated in the EYFS. He took in children from 3 years of age in preparation for elementary school. Froebel returned to Keilhau in 1837 and it was here that he began to work on his central ideas for 'gifts' and 'occupations'. In 1839 his wife died and he moved yet again, to Blankenburg, a small town not far from Oberweissbach, where he was born. There he taught classes of thirty to forty 1- to 7-year-olds. It was at Blankenburg that he decided on the name 'kindergarten'. As Weston says, the word kindergarten 'cleverly combines the human (kinder) with the natural (garten), and can mean both garden *of* children and garden *for* children' (2000: 15).

In 1844 Froebel published what many consider to be his most influential book, *Mutter, Spiel und Koselieder* (Mother, Play and Nursery Songs). These songs were in the vernacular and echo Comenius's view that to develop a sense of self and nation the mother tongue was all-important. (See Figure 5.2, which is a rhyme in German about a bird's nest. Froebel invites us with the words, *Kommt, lasst uns unsern Kindern leben!* This translates as, Come, let us live for our children.) As well as encouraging Germany to develop its own sense of nationhood, Froebel's intention was also to show mothers that their role was a vocational one, beginning at birth. This emphasis on the mother as central to a child's early education is a powerful theme in the work of Comenius, Pestalozzi and Froebel. Froebel set up training courses for teachers and what is highly significant is that these teachers were all women. Froebel has sometimes been criticized for this over-emphasis on women as educators of young children. However, it is clear that this was strongly influenced by his own childhood experience of being deprived of a caring mother. Pound shows that in his writing he indicated that the death of his mother had a huge impact on the whole of his future development (2005).

In 1848, when revolutions swept across Europe, there were more than fifty kindergartens operating in Germany. His old military acquaintances, Middendorff and Langethal, continued to support him, lecturing alongside him in Frankfurt, Dresden and Hamburg. They also published his ideas in a

Figure 5.2   Friedrich Froebel: Kommt, lasst uns unsern Kindern leben!

weekly paper which circulated from 1837 to 1840. In 1851 the Prussian govern-ment banned all kindergartens as seditious, and neighbouring states followed suit. Oppressive governments were nervous of a method which promoted freedom, and many believed that the employment of women as kindergarten instructors threatened to undermine the family (Weston 2000). One can only imagine the despair Froebel must have felt in the light of these reactions to his life's work. Nevertheless, 1848 saw Froebel marry again, this time to a former pupil who continued his work after his death in 1852.

Implication of his ideas in practice

Froebel took Pestalozzi's ideas and changed them to fit his own theories. While the focus of kindergarten practice was based on the 'object lesson', the Froebelian object lesson was much more symbolic than Pestalozzi's. Gutek (1972) suggests that Froebel believed that the objects presented to the children were a part of God's creation and therefore imbued with spirituality, a clear example of religious belief running alongside a developing scientific approach to learning. These carefully selected objects had the potential, in his view, to awaken a potential for learning already present in the child and these objects were divinely given to meet the children's needs. Gutek further illustrates this viewpoint in the following examples of children's work with elemental materials such as sand, clay and water:

> When the child is playing with water he wants to see his own image reflected 'in order to glimpse his soul' . . . children's occupation with sand and clay reveals a desire to experience the plastic element of life and to shape and master raw materials.
>
> (Gutek 1972: 230)

Like Comenius and Pestalozzi before him, Froebel did not agree with Rousseau's view that nature was enough in itself; the guiding hand of a trained, sympathetic and loving educator was essential to enable the children to make links and connections in their learning, a view I would share wholeheartedly. Froebel's gifts were, according to nature's laws, presented to the child at the moment when they were ready to receive their inherent wisdom. While this approach stays close to Pestalozzi's reified vision of nature it also adds a strong spiritual dimension, the gifts taking the form of symbolic geometric shapes. The ball or sphere, for example, represented the unity of the universe. Froebel devoted his time at Blankenburg to developing these gifts in his practical work with the children. This notion of unity was central to his philosophy: the unity of all things which came from God. He believed that God is everything and everything is God. This Romantic notion of unity and connectedness is also

Figure 5.3   Froebel's Spielplatz Blankenburg (postcard)

reflected in his garden structures (see Figure 5.3), which he designed himself in the early days.

The four rectangular boundaries of the garden were worked by the whole school community, adult and children alike, to grow vegetables and flowers. (The activity of gardening was one of Froebel's most important 'occupations' and, as mentioned in the previous chapter, is becoming a strong feature of current outdoor practice.) The produce was sold and used by the community. Each of the small inner plots belonged to individual children and was clearly labelled with their name. They had the freedom to grow whatever they wished there (Lawrence 1952). The structure of the garden reflected the unity of the community, all working together and connecting within the structure, while still preserving their own individual freedom to explore and develop their understanding of nature. In so doing they would grow closer to their understanding of God. White (1909) argues that the strict scientific regularity of this structure can also be seen as a reaction against the post-war chaos of the time. The design clearly reflects Pestalozzi and Froebel's prerequisite for effective learning, namely a safe, secure environment. It also illustrates Froebel's desire to protect the child's creative potential from untrained, outside forces. He believed that the outcome of the child's work in his own garden would be a true reflection of the child's own nature.

Another prominent feature of his 'occupations', in addition to gardening and looking after animals, were daily excursions into the surrounding countryside, towns, forests and farms so that the children could experience at first hand their oneness with nature. Herrington describes these activities, which took the form of, for example:

> Categorizing natural and artificial objects having similar forms, observing the physical layout of a town as a reflection of its social formation, following a stream from its mountain origin to its river descent, and comparing children's growth to the growth of plants . . . [while he] consistently stressed the reverent capacity of the unknowable in these experiences.
>
> (Herrington 2001: 33)

Froebel's legacy

Lawrence claims that although the term 'child-centred' is a modern term its original conception can be traced back to Froebel. I would argue that we can go back even further, to Owen, Rousseau, Pestalozzi and Comenius for the emergence of this notion. Equally, these pioneers shared with Froebel the view that childhood was something sacred and of great value. Along with them, Froebel brings to the present day the awareness of the importance of the education of young children; children learn through sensory experiences, play, movement and meaningful tasks, and they should be supported by highly trained, receptive adults.

Herrington (2001: 45) argues that landscape architecture and the kindergarten grew out of the same Romantic perspective, when 'gardens and landscapes were designed to provide epiphanic experiences with nature'. Wordsworth (1770–1850), the great English Romantic poet, clearly illustrates this view in his poem 'The Tables Turned' (1798), suggesting that one moment of communion with nature can teach us more than all the rational, scientific thinking prevalent in his time:

> One impulse from a vernal wood
> May teach you more of man
> Of moral evil and of good
> Than all the sages can.

Despite the fact that Froebel's mystical notion of the garden as a spiritual space has generally become submerged by the obsession with targets in our present educational 'audit culture', there are still traces of 'awe and wonder' in our early years curriculum. These are particularly evident in the birth to

3 section of the EYFS, where practitioners are invited to 'encourage young children to explore puddles, trees and surfaces such as grass, concrete or pebbles' (DfES 2007a: 85) or conduct '. . . investigations of the natural world . . . bubbles to investigate the effects of the wind' (DfES 2007a: 77). Sadly, though, these examples are all laced with learning outcomes and the sheer joy of experiencing these activities takes second place.

Nonetheless, spaces of 'awe and wonder' still exist in our built spaces today. In fact the range of reflective spaces and gardens that we see today can be seen as embracing some of Froebel's ideas, for example therapeutic gardens, land art and memorial gardens. The work of Andrew Goldsworthy (1956–present), a sculptor, environmentalist and photographer who works in Scotland, comes to mind, as that of someone exquisitely fusing nature and art in his land forms. These are specifically created in natural and urban settings to draw out the unique character of specific landscapes (Donovan and Fiske 2010).

Froebel's argument that children learn outdoors through contact with nature is strongly evident in the current Swedish *Skogsmulle, I Ur och Skur* and UK Forest School practice, as will be seen in later chapters. His biggest legacy and accompaniment to this, however, has to be the importance of movement and play as features of young children's learning. This notion, although evident in all the current prescriptive literature, is often sadly lacking or misunderstood, in particular for 4-year-olds in full-time reception classes, where literacy and numeracy take precedence. This is particularly apparent for young boys, in this restrictive environment. The need for young children to spend time outside each day is a strong recommendation in the EYFS documentation. However, sadly it is not a state obligation; economic considerations once again take precedence over children's well-being. This is because making outdoor learning statutory would inhibit the private sector as they would be obliged to acquire premises with outdoor facilities. It can only be hoped that whatever little time these children do spend outside will involve some contact with nature, if only with the sky and the weather.

Snicgoski (1994) notes that John Dewey (1859–1952) argued that the principles underlying Froebel's philosophy of development had no basis in science whatsoever. By the end of the nineteenth century, new intellectual trends in educational thinking, particularly Darwin's theory of evolutionary naturalism, challenged the principles underpinning Froebel's philosophy of education. Nonetheless, Dewey was later to play an important role in adapting Froebel's theories to a more measurable, scientific model. John Dewey, the philosopher, psychologist and educationalist, in fact based most of his work on Froebel's ideas. He agreed with Froebel that development came from within the child and that socialization and the environment mattered. They both believed that moral and intellectual freedom could be gained by self-activity. Dewey adopted the 'object lesson' initiated by Pestalozzi and developed by Froebel. However, as an educator who based his views on the growing body of scientific expertise in the field, he did not share Froebel's mystical and symbolic understandings of the objects. Dewey adapted many of Froebel's ideas on outdoor learning: he adapted the excursions, for example, to become nature walks where the children learned to identify, classify and name plants and birds. In dismissing Froebel's 'revelatory' nature of these excursions, Dewey replaced them with 'a digestible system for memorization' (Herrington 2001: 43). Here we can see the beginning of a process of teaching central to our current audit culture: a scientific system where we only teach what supposedly can be measured and tested.

Influences and links with other pioneers

Froebel shared with Pestalozzi the view that each child is innately good and both men valued what originated from the child, seeing this as a necessary starting point for learning. This was in complete contrast to the contemporary view that a child's nature needs to be repressed. The role of the adult as mediator here becomes of great importance. Froebel, like Pestalozzi, understood that if children were to make the necessary connections in their learning by being in nature, exploring its properties and elemental qualities, they needed well-qualified educators who could make this happen. Froebel advocated that kindergartens should be run by 'trained child gardeners' who naturally followed on from the mother's role (Lawrence 1952: 195). Older notions were not, however, completely absent, and in the 'occupations' there is a distinct suggestion of needing to keep control, the child needing to be kept busy lest it succumb to baser instincts. Below the Romantic view of the child as 'good', the older notion that the child is evil is still just below the surface. The fear remains that, unless guided by an adult, the child will revert to evil, just as the untended garden will eventually return to the wild. Froebel also accepted Pestalozzi's notion of child freedom and the importance of emotional security, but Froebel was 'much more prone to symbolic and mystical interpretation of the child's behaviour' (Gutek 1972: 213).

Froebel himself took part in the training process in Pestalozzi's method at Yverdun. He extended this in his own work. At Keilhau his school was organized as an educational community. Parents were involved and specialist training became established. In 1849 he opened a training college at Marienthal where the students studied for a full year so that they could experience and learn the activities which needed to be carried out with the children in each season. Like Pestalozzi, he became an educational lobbyist, bending the ear of kings and politicians, as well as lecturing in local towns and nearby cities. His writing, particularly *The Education of Man* (*Die Menschenerziehung*) (1826) and *Mother Songs* (*Mutter, Spiel und Koselieder*) (1844), was well received, and helped spread word of his new system in German-speaking countries.

The failed revolutions of 1848 unsettled European governments, however, which, in their growing conservatism, became less receptive to educational methods seen to be 'nurturing future revolutionaries' (Liebschner 1991: ix). The Prussian government edict of *Kindergarten Verbot* (1851) banning kindergartens as subversive, was not rescinded until 1860. Froebel's kindergarten movement ironically benefited from this ban as his ideas spread internationally, due to the widespread emigration of liberal-minded Germans from a repressive Germany to America and the Western European countries. Some went to England where 'their ideas appealed to rich, middle-class, public spirited, cultured Manchester merchants and the like, who cared about education for their own children and for those of the proletariat' (Lawrence 1952: 11).

Froebel's doctrine appealed to many civil reform groups active at the time in Britain, such as those fighting for higher education for women. The Home and Colonial Infant School Society had already been set up in 1837 to train teachers of 2- to 6-year-old children in Pestalozzi's method (Lawrence 1952; Browne 2004). This Society stressed the specific needs of young children as being different from those of older children, requiring specialist training. This was in opposition to the contemporary view that no training was required for this purpose and schools could be set up by anyone who could 'mother' young children.

The Froebel movement was given further prestige by the patronage of interested, titled personages such as Baroness Bertha von Marenholz-Bulow, a member of an aristocratic family connected with the Humboldts. She became an active promoter of Froebelian methods in England, Ireland and Europe. Educational reformers such as Owen had already helped consolidate the idea of infant schools. The Manchester Froebel Society was formed in 1873 and the London equivalent in 1874. By 1876 the Societies had established teachers' training with an accredited diploma and an inspectorate designed to protect Froebel's method from misinterpretation and abuse. The Froebel Educational Institute was established in 1894 in London with an attached Demonstration Kindergarten to support this training. This was originally at Colet Gardens but then moved to Challoner Street (see Figure 5.4).

Like Pestalozzi before them, both the London and Manchester Societies became educational lobbyists, petitioning parliament on a range of issues. They influenced the Educational Code of 1881, a government initiative which focused on payment by results as an efficient and cheap way of educating the masses. An example of what this meant in practice can be seen in Curtis's (1948) example of the installation of horizontal and parallel bars in asphalt school playgrounds, the outcome of which was that 'owing to the large number of accidents [they] were subsequently removed' (p. 298). The Societies sent a deputation to Whitehall to Anthony John Mundella, Vice President of the Education Department and strong supporter of the cause of popular education.

Figure 5.4 Miss Evelyn Hope-Wallace with her class at Challoner Street School 1903–04

The Societies won Mundella's support and as a consequence there was a gradual move away from the narrowness of the payment by results system and its restricted curriculum. All classes in state elementary schools now had to include 'simple lessons on objects and the phenomena of nature and common life', a feature central to the Froebelian approach (Liebschner 1991). This was a considerable achievement at a time when the 3Rs totally dominated the curriculum. Mundella went on to become something of a convert, delivering lectures promoting Froebelian principles. Lobbying by means of deputation to ministers became a feature of Society activity thereafter. In a later example, in 1922 the Froebel Societies argued against the use of untrained teachers in infant schools (a supposed economy measure of the time) (Lawrence 1952). The same lobbying, for the same issue, continues to this day.

Working within the monitorial model, provision for popular education in the first half of the nineteenth century was dominated by two voluntary groups, the National Society and the British and Foreign School Society. A combination of education to meet economic 'needs' (usually ill-thought-out ones at that and woefully short-term), and of education on the cheap, has dominated most government thinking from nineteenth-century developments down to the present day. These groups could not continue to meet the growing demands of mass education and in 1833 the government intervened (Bowen 1981: 291). Education from that point on became increasingly regulated. For example, Kay-Shuttleworth's teacher–pupil model was already evolving out of the monitorial system. This development illustrates what over the long term has continued to be the pragmatic and utilitarian practice of government in Britain, where the interests of economy overrode pedagogic innovation in the provision of mass education. The marketized model, then as now, was adopted as the simplest and most cost-efficient way to educate the majority. The total incompatibility of running a business and educating in the same venture are persuasively outlined by Moss in his article 'There are alternatives!' (2009).

Pestalozzi's ideas were mediated historically not just by Froebel alone. Johann Friedrich Herbart (1776–1841), a contemporary of Froebel and an educational philosopher, was also working on Pestalozzi's ideas at this time. He adapted the main stereotypical features of Pestalozzianism and Froebelianism such as the object lesson and the occupations, reducing them to 'mechanical craft exercises in paper folding and cutting as well as activities such as shop work and needlework, preparing children for the assembly line' (Bowen 1981: 350). Herbart dismissed the mysticism and pantheism inherent in their approach, focusing instead on the main goal of education, which he perceived as character formation. This approach suited government in the early nineteenth century as an efficient, low-cost method of mass education. Herbart's ideas flourished in Western Europe and the USA because of their scientific approach. This 'fitted well with the technological, inventive practical ethos of an America trying to build a new progressive society' (Bowen 1981: 350).

Froebel and Pestalozzi's ideas also influenced Uno Cygnaeus (1810–88), a Finnish educator and major proponent of manual learning. Gutek explains how Cygnaeus influenced Swedish government policy in making it compulsory for boys in rural schools to study a combination of Froebel's gifts and occupations alongside practical subjects, like metalwork and wood carving. This system was promoted in Swedish schools under the name of 'sloyd' (a handicraft-based education) by the educator Otto Salomon (1849–1907).

Although educational reformers such as Mathew Arnold (1822–88) strongly challenged the limitations of the payment by results approach to learning, he was only successful in reducing some of its worst excesses. Clearly, this was not the time for an organic, holistic approach to learning, with small classes where children were seen as individuals. The philosophy of nature and unity was in total opposition to *laissez-faire* individualism and the economic exploitation of nature that was so evident in industrialization. Froebel and Pestalozzi's ideas went into a long period of gestation, re-emerging in changed economic and political times.

Their real breakthrough came in the 1920s with Margaret McMillan (1860–1931), a member of the Froebel Society. The context for this breakthrough was the government's concern for the state of the nation's health after the First World War. Outdoor learning came into its own again when the state opened nurseries in gardens designed to create healthy future citizens. These nurseries reflected an increasing concern with environmental influences on health and behaviour, especially among the urban population. Such concerns had in fact been evident from the late nineteenth century, and were reflected in a new concern with the poor of great cities, above all the East End of London. From this time reports and commissions on the state of the poor and of their education proliferated. By returning to nature and its potential for learning in the outdoors Pestalozzi and Froebel can be seen as part of a counter-current that has eventually become part of modern educational theory.

Figure 5.5 traces the influences which shaped Pestalozzi, Froebel and current thinking. It also makes some predictions as to which factors may influence the future.

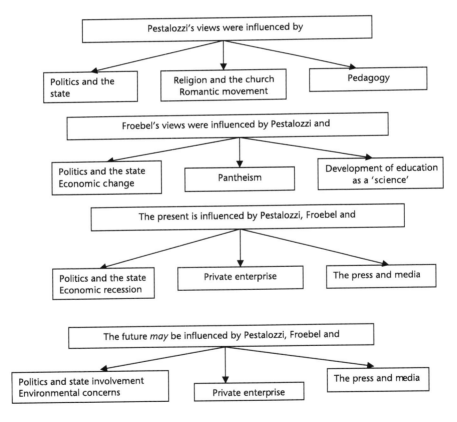

Figure 5.5 Pestalozzi's inheritance and legacy as mediated through Froebel

Reflective question

- Look at Figure 5.5. Plot a similar structure tracing back the influences on your personal formation and practice. Share with a small group and consider what the future influences might be.

6   Born to breathe: Margaret McMillan (1860–1931)

Figure 6.1 Margaret McMillan

Education and society in the time of McMillan

Margaret McMillan brought children's health to the foreground of thinking about education. She believed that in order to get the most from education children needed to be clean, healthy and well nourished. They should have a good environment where they could breathe freely, a situation not possible for the majority of young children, especially those living in the foul air of the London slums. This became her passion and led to a number of significant reforms in her lifetime. Her view can be seen in the context of a nation in shock following the First World War but also the furore that followed the recruitment of working men for the Boer War between 1899 and 1902. Forty to 60 per cent of them were found to be unfit for active service (Bradburn 1989; Steedman 1990). Education was seen to be the best way to redress this and create healthy citizens for the future. Reforms were put in place and the physical development of children through games and exercises became the norm in schools, while military drill became a recognized means of maintaining discipline.

Since compulsory education was introduced in 1870 the needs of the poor in elementary schools were more visible now than ever before. Although children were protected by law from the worst factory practices and education was available to all over the age of 5, many were still unable to take full advantage of it since they were still working half-time in the mills. Too hungry and exhausted to study at school, they would often fall asleep at their desks (Lowndes 1960). McMillan campaigned for change in 1895, leading a deputation to lobby the Home Secretary, Lord Asquith. The age limit for half-time work was raised from 11 to 12 but the practice continued, and was not finally abolished until 1922. Many working-class parents strongly opposed this reform since children were seen as important contributors to the family budget as well as investments for the future. Many mill owners were also in opposition, claiming that such a reform would jeopardize the future of economic trade.

This example can be seen against a background of strategies which were prevalent in the late nineteenth and early twentieth century. Working-class children were viewed as vulnerable and in need of protection. The government became involved and early intervention was seen as the only way to counter 'neglect' and produce better citizens, the alternative, it was supposed, being neglected children who would inevitably become criminalized and a burden on society. An interesting parallel today is the report by the government think tank Demos and commissioned by Barnados, which posits a similar argument regarding children in care. Earlier state involvement in education represented a general move to state intervention, seen in family life and personal morality (for example, homosexuality was criminalized at this time). Problems which would have previously been described as private or the concerns of the free market now became part of a collective, *social* problem which entailed more regulation (Chen 2003).

Public gardens and parks had earlier evolved as a means of managing class relations in the new urban, industrial environments of Victorian England. Gardening metaphors subsequently became a popular way of understanding social problems among middle-class reformers. They believed that the environment in which the child was reared, like the garden, was of paramount importance. The street, for example, was seen as 'an inappropriate space for . . . children, since it brought them into contact with evil . . . undesirable homes were regarded as most detrimental to the development of children's character' (Chen 2003: 470). Chen adds that gardening metaphors portrayed parents as gardeners and compared children to plants in the garden of the family, so that 'parents and children themselves [were] simultaneously the ruled and agents of the enterprise of making good citizens' (p. 475). McMillan's garden, as an environment for growing children and educating parents, was part of this interest in the 'social garden'. However, her Christian socialist views separated her from the paternalism so often inherent in the garden metaphor. Her aim was to create a more equal society where everyone, rich or poor, could attain a good education and standard of living.

Bradburn (1989) informs us that McMillan was familiar with the work of Owen, Pestalozzi and Rousseau. Many of these books she read in their original language in the British Museum, in London. McMillan also knew the work of the French physician Jean Marc Gaspard Itard (1751–1838), and shared his concern that some effects of early disadvantage might be difficult to retrieve. She was familiar with Montessori's work with the poor in San Lorenzo and the influence of Itard's pupil Edouard Seguin (1812–80). McMillan was particularly drawn to Seguin's ideas. These featured prominently in her work, not simply because of his methods, which she interpreted differently from Montessori, but also because of his attention to the health and well-being of the poor. He 'advocated garden schools in obedience to axioms of Physiological Education in order to make the schooling of the masses more active and practical': this involved exercises designed to strengthen the physical body and develop sensory-motor co-ordination (Steedman 1990: 96). His work also stressed the huge importance of self-reliance and independence. These ideas became central to McMillan's work. She also shared his view that 'to make the child feel that he [sic] is loved, and to make him feel eager to love in his turn, is the end of our teaching as it has been its beginning' (Bradburn 1989: 58). 'Love' was a feature essential to teaching and learning for McMillan as well as Montessori, Owen, Froebel, Pestalozzi and Comenius. Her sister Rachel's axiom was, 'Educate every child as if he were your own' (McMillan 1919: 24). Such explicit expressions of love as a feature of teaching and learning are not used in current statutory early years documentation and their absence should be questioned. The closest one gets to this is the use of the word 'respect', which appears in the EYFS. Here it appears in Personal, Social and Emotional Development in relation to behaviour towards others. 'Love' and 'business' do not indeed seem to mix very readily.

In the years leading up to the First World War, Britain led the way in progressive education. Froebel's ideas were popular once again, as were Montessori's. (McMillan became an active member of the Council of the Froebel Society.) Bowen (1981) argues that progressivism was a product of the continuing middle-class enthusiasm for voluntary, secular provision, outside the dominating hand of church or state. He notes that theosophical and anthroposophical supporters played a large part in the progressive movement. However, as the state increasingly legislated school codes, levied taxes and provided schools and trained teachers, voluntary activity was sidelined and 'progressivism' became more evident in state thinking. State intervention and control began to impinge seriously on independent provision, and on opportunities to put innovative ideas into practice.

Knowledge and professionalism became apparent in scientific developments in the fields of physiology and psychology. More spiritual readings of these developments were apparent in Rudolf Steiner (1861–1925). His pansophical theories were in tune with many of McMillan's beliefs regarding play and personal and social development, especially his view that the child was a spiritual being in readiness for awakening by the environment. Meanwhile, Susan Isaacs (1885–1948) was promoting the importance of free 'unfettered' outdoor play at the Malting House School in Cambridge, using a psychology-based approach as an alternative to Montessori. Her approach depended on observation and reflection as strategies for exploring the importance of children's social and emotional development. McMillan was more explicitly political than the other innovators. Her political beliefs were deeply embedded in socialism, as were Owen's. As a member of the Independent Labour Party (ILP) and the Fabian Society she strongly believed in the brotherhood of man and the creation of a new society through the promotion of health and education of young children. Her philosophy was integral to her socialism but so was her Christianity. This was illustrated by her membership of the Christian Socialist Movement, which was founded in 1848.

The early life and development of McMillan

McMillan was born in New York in 1860. Like Comenius, Pestalozzi and Froebel before her, she lost a parent when she was just a child. This was compounded by further personal loss when her sister Elizabeth died in the same year, 1865. She also contracted scarlet fever as a child and lost her hearing from the age of 3 to 14. She recalls how she never actually heard her father's voice and only heard her mother's when her hearing spontaneously returned. Bradburn argues that this may, in part, explain McMillan's later obsession with the 'voice', both as a persuasive orator on the streets of Bradford and London and as an educator in the slums. Her dream was that every child should be a speaker and 'grownups would possess voices full of subtle intonations which would make conversation quite a delightful thing' (1989: 78). According to Steedman, McMillan believed that the human voice was a key factor in how people perceived class. While Owen saw no opportunities for civil discourse in the crowded slums of the working class, McMillan felt that this could be resolved by working within the school community of parents and children.

McMillan believed her first five years in New York were probably the happiest of her life. When recalling her memories of childhood in America in her *Life of Rachel McMillan* (1927: 8–9), she described the house where she lived with her family: 'The wooden house is a mere shelter in summer. It seems less like a house than a kind of roofed series of gateways opening on the wide sunlit world.' It is easy here to see the source of McMillan's future design for the shelters in her children's garden. Shelters such as these are still evident today in Forest Schools and *I Ur och Skur* settings in Sweden. After her father's death the family moved to Scotland to live with her grandparents, who were members of the Free High Church. This was an open-minded institution concerned with social justice and was to be a strong influence on her future socialist views. She was educated at the High School and Royal Academy in Inverness. Her father, himself an advocate for social reform, first emigrated to America because of his political beliefs, more particularly his anti-landlordism.

As part of her training to be a governess, McMillan's 'enlightened' family sent her to study music and learn the language in Frankfurt. Here she came into contact with contemporary European ideas and, in particular, the philosophy and socialist theories of Karl Marx (1818–83), the German philosopher and revolutionary. She went on to teach English and learn French in Geneva, the birthplace of Jean-Jacques Rousseau. Bradburn notes that many of her fellow students were themselves exiled, refugees from Russia and Germany. These experiences abroad clearly influenced her politically.

McMillan then moved to London to be with her sister Rachel, who introduced her to the Fabian Society. This was the intellectual wing of the Labour Movement and included ardent socialists and champions of the working class such as George Bernard Shaw (1856–1950), and Sidney Webb (1859–1947) and his wife Beatrice (1858–1943). McMillan and her sister joined the Independent Labour Party (ILP). Here she met and became a close friend of Keir Hardie (1856–1915), a self-taught Scottish miner and a Christian socialist like herself. He was a founding member of the ILP, which later became a part of the Labour Party. She began to speak on public platforms demanding reforms for the poor. She spoke, for example, on behalf of the dockers in the London Dock Strike of 1889 or 'The Tanner Strike' as it came to be called. Her employer at the time was one Lady Meux, a rags-to-riches barmaid and actress who had inherited a large fortune but was still shunned by middle-class society. McMillan became her companion. Lady Meux saw in her the potential to become a great actress and paid for her training. She was most displeased, however, at McMillan's public display of socialist views. McMillan stood up for her principles and left Lady Meux's employment, despite her lack of financial means. Personal sacrifice such as this was not uncommon in the early days of socialism among members of the Labour Movement.

She became renowned for her persuasive oratory and was invited to Bradford where she was elected to join the School Board. She remained there from 1893 to 1902. McMillan, the only woman on the Board, seized every opportunity to outline her educational plans. Her key messages stressed the pressing need for women to be educated, particularly since they, as mothers, were the first educators. Bradburn claims that McMillan saw in the Labour Movement a way of translating into reality her vision for creating a better society. Her work in Bradford highlighted the severe poverty of the slum children, 'facets of industrial life normally swept under the carpet by upper and middle classes' (Lowndes 1960: 95). She actively campaigned for health reforms to counter the appalling poverty around her. As a way of forcing the wealthy to understand the implications of this poverty, McMillan presented the working-class child as a threat to their well-being. Not only were these children innocent in their poverty, they were also corrupted by it and a threat to society. Coupled with concerns about the Boer War and the poor physique of the nation, poor children's ill-health, she claimed, 'threatened Britain's imperial prowess' (Steedman 1990: 67). Her words struck home.

McMillan returned to London in 1902 where her sister Rachel was now a trained sanitary inspector and hygiene teacher. Bradburn describes the main issues which dominated the political agenda at this time: '. . . free trade and imperialism, state regulation and *laissez-faire*, policies of social welfare, a quest for better wages for workers and women's claim for emancipation' (1989: 66). It is against this backdrop that we have to see McMillan's drive for education and health reforms. In her case the search for greater efficiency was not motivated by any desire to create wealth but by her passion to work towards a more just and humane society.

In 1905 she was elected as a member of the National Administrative Council of the ILP, alongside other well-known socialists such as her friend Keir Hardie, Emmeline Pankhurst (1857–1928), the leader of the British Suffragette Movement, and Ramsay MacDonald (1866–1937), who was later to become the first British Labour Prime Minister in 1924. McMillan and her sister both supported the universal suffrage movement. Although she had little in the way of financial resources, McMillan had enormous resourcefulness and political nous. She placed herself right at the centre of the push for political reform.

Like her parents, McMillan went on to demonstrate her own concern for social justice. She worked tirelessly with her sister Rachel to improve the life chances of young children exposed to ill-health and poor diet in the streets and slums of Deptford, just as Montessori was doing in Rome and Owen had been in New Lanark nearly one hundred years before. Her efforts and those of other reformers at the time saw the first school medical inspections in 1899. Although she met a great deal of opposition as her views were considered to undermine parental responsibility, the provision of free school meals for the poor was on the statute book by 1906.

McMillan and her sister went on to set up outdoor Night Camps and a Camp School in Deptford to offset the poverty and unhealthy living conditions of the slum children. Government legislation was now paving the way for a healthier nation, starting with school-age children. McMillan argued that these reforms were futile if the health of the pre-school child was not considered. By 1917 the Rachel McMillan Nursery School was opened with one hundred children on the roll.

Implication of her ideas in practice

In her preface to *The Nursery School* (1919), McMillan clearly states her vision of the role of education for the very young: 'This book was written in order to urge the nation to set vigorously about the salvation of many.' McMillan was of particular importance in this drive for reform in that she included middle-class children in her brief. She believed that wealthy parents also needed help in nurturing their children, which was a task normally handed over to a nursemaid. She notes that 'to one [child] we may have to offer baths and towels, to the other the chance of making his pinafore dirty' (McMillan 1919). She believed that all children had the right to equal standards of care and questioned whether 'the average mother', regardless of her economic circumstances, was capable of supplying this (pp. 22–3). In her view, there was an additional need for all children to have trained nurses to 'nurture' them. This was a striking departure from contemporary thinking and a challenge to middle-class perceptions of themselves as role models for the working class. Up until 1905 children under the age of 5 were attending elementary schools, despite the school starting age being set at 5. The provision was deemed inappropriate by a Board of Education inspection and from that time on under-5s were excluded from elementary schools. Parents were forced to rely on voluntary provision for their children, or else leave them to life on the streets (Curtis 1848; Board of Education 1905; Curtis 1948). Concern among reformers for the welfare of these children began to grow, and with good reason. The first medical inspection in Bradford, according to Lowndes (1960), revealed that 'over one hundred of the children had not had their clothes off for six to eight months' (p. 57). This explains the urgency McMillan attached to having baths as a central feature of provision. Her ideal was for children, of all ages, to have a daily bath, as well as daily breathing exercises to offset disease and infection.

In McMillan's view, conditions in state schools at this time left much to be desired. It was her opinion that 'compulsory schooling meant compulsory contact with every form of disease' (Bradburn 1989: 49). She had her own vision for change which was informed by visits to many London primary schools, having become a manager of a group of schools in Deptford. This vision, clearly outlined in Table 6.1, was her model for nursery schools. She saw this as suitable for all schools, starting with the youngest and moving up to the oldest. This 'bottom-up' vision is in total contrast to the 'top-down' model which currently dominates educational provision and practice.

Table 6.1   McMillan's vision for reform of state schools. Adapted from Bradburn (1989: 175)

State school provision	McMillan's vision for reform
Schools surrounded by asphalt yards	Schools to be set in large gardens
Schools were prison-like, poorly ventilated with poor sanitation	Schools should be open-air buildings with good sanitation
Schools were full of dirty, sick children	Schools should attend to the health, hygiene and nourishment of children
Schools had large classes using authoritarian discipline	Schools should have smaller classes, be friendly and informal
Children were taught as a whole class and silence was the norm	Children should be taught as individuals and encouraged to speak and listen
Schools were subject-centred, mainly based on the three Rs	Schools should be child-centred with a holistic, empirical approach to learning
Schools did not welcome parents	Parents should be welcomed as the child's first educators

Improved ventilation and sanitation were Victorian obsessions, the early twentieth century seeing the emergence of the Open Air School Movement. These schools were designed to prevent the spread of tuberculosis, so combining education with medical care. McMillan's Camp Schools were also set up at this time. Steedman (1990) argues, however, that McMillan's schools were quite different from those in the Open Air Movement, which removed children from their homes. Like Pestalozzi, McMillan believed that keeping children within their family community was central to their well-being. The Open Air Movement went into decline with the invention of antibiotics after the Second World War.

While in Bradford many of her reforms began to be introduced. Less formal individual teaching began to take place and nature study became an active part of the curriculum, alongside visits to local parks and school trips (Bradburn 1989). Like Montessori, McMillan's philosophy was based on a deep Christian belief which viewed the outdoor environment as a place that would enable children to discover themselves. This can also be seen in the wider context of a growing interest and great debate in the development of garden cities such as, for example, Welwyn Garden City in Hertfordshire. Gardens in large conurbations would enable people, rich and poor alike, to breathe more freely, exercise and enjoy the beauty of nature. People were to be free in designated wild areas but also influenced by more controlled floral displays of popular mass colour plantings (Elliott 1986). This could also be seen as a visual representation of man untamed and tamed. The garden at this time was becoming a space representing order and design as well as freedom. It was coming to be seen, as Steedman says, 'as a mediator between populations, industry and culture' (1990: 97).

Like Owen and Montessori, McMillan's main aim was to improve the physical and emotional well-being of children. She held the view that these were necessary prerequisites to intellectual development. She believed in the need for a planned environment outdoors, as Montessori did, where the children engaged in purposeful play, with freedom of choice and movement. However, she differed significantly from Montessori in her approach, which was less didactic and encompassed imaginative play. This was a feature absent in Montessori's philosophy. In the early days of the Camp Schools McMillan faced a lot of opposition from parents who feared for their children's safety when sleeping outdoors at night. Would such a school be at all possible now? My own experience suggests otherwise, playing outside in the rain in winter or spending an afternoon in the woods being viewed as impossible (Joyce 2006).

The school was a garden with shelters, which she used to develop Seguin's ideas of creating opportunities for sensory experiences. She used outdoor play as a teaching and learning tool to offset the damage already done where 'children had their senses dulled if not perverted. Some of the young babies already knew the taste of ale, vinegar and even pickles' (Bradburn 1989). McMillan clearly disapproved of these strong-tasting foodstuffs. The school was in full view of the home and served a dual purpose. Parents could see their children, knowing they were safe and happy, while at the same time they could learn from the practices they observed. This was one of McMillan's key themes. The school was an integral part of the community, as it is with the Reggio approach to learning. Educating the parents was an important feature of this as a way of helping them to understand and realize what was possible for their children. She believed they desperately needed this help to free them from what she referred to in *The Nursery School* (1919: 182) as their 'imprison[ment] in a kind of loving ignorance'. She went on to explain: 'A Nursery school is, or should be, a part of the home life. Ours is overlooked by a hundred windows, and often there is a crowd of eager faces at each . . . The Nursery is for them a kind of return to the outdoor theatre, it is an open space, a garden, a school' (p. 29). McMillan continued, noting that once the children were inside the garden they 'come under the influence of the great healers, earth, sun, air, sleep and joy . . . It is a point of honour with us to make every child so well that he needs no doctor' (p. 31).

Camp Schools were surrounded by beautiful gardens. These were seen as an oasis in a sea of greyness (Lowndes 1960). Using whatever resources were at hand, such as banana crates for the babies to sleep in, she recycled and reused whatever she could find (Bradburn 1989). (See Figures 6.2 and 6.3 for an illustration of this.) She was helped by friends and philanthropists such as Joseph Fels (1853–1914), an American millionaire who made his fortune from producing Naphalta soap. Many visitors to the garden schools described with great enthusiasm what they encountered. One such visitor reported as follows: 'Squalid, dilapidated buildings, the sickly children playing listlessly in the street . . . passed through a gate to . . . a veritable paradise. The contrast was overwhelming. A beautiful space, garden, trees, grass, flowers, sunshine and brilliant colour . . . dispelled depression' (Lowndes 1960: 79).

The First World War (1914–18) brought many difficulties in its train. It shattered McMillan's hopes for a better world and the brotherhood of nations. She opened her doors to the children and babies of munitions workers, this childcare being funded by the government. There was a serious shortage of staff since many trained teachers and nurses were recruited to the armed forces. Not only was the quality of care in her outdoor schools greatly diminished but the constant fear of air raids and zeppelin attacks made her work impossible. Again the question of risk springs to mind here and the total impossibility of such a project in the present day. When the war ended, so too did the funding for the children of the munitions workers and numbers began to diminish. These were desperate times for the McMillan sisters and the pressure began to take its toll on Rachel's health. She died in 1917 aged 58, one year before the first nursery school opened in her name.

Figure 6.2 Children playing with munitions boxes in the Rachel McMillan Nursery School, 1945

Figure 6.3 Children sleeping outdoors in homemade beds made from recycled materials, 1920s

McMillan's legacy

McMillan's vision for children met the government's needs of the day for a healthy citizenry as an investment for the future workforce. Her attention to health and well-being is a central feature of her legacy today. The current provision of Children's Centres, combining education and care, is testament to this influence. Her emphasis on the cognitive value of everyday experiences and their contribution to children's health contributed greatly to today's theory and practice. McMillan valued activities such as bathing, for example, as personal, social and physical learning experiences. Following Seguin's teaching she advocated that from the age of 3 children should be encouraged to wash and dress themselves (McMillan 1919). These personal, independence skills are integral to current documentation within the EYFS but they are no longer valued as learning experiences central to nursery and school practice since they require a lot of time and patience on the part of the adult and the child. Time for such activities is sadly not a feature of our target-driven culture.

McMillan's view of parents as the first educators is central to current provision, as was her view that parents needed to be involved in their children's learning if the outcomes were to be successful. This was a strong feature of my own practice in the pre-audit culture of 1990 when the Rumbold Report (DES 1990) was the only guidance available for practitioners in the early years. The Effective Provision of Pre-school Education (EPPE) Project (Sylva et al. 2004) also strongly supports this view. McMillan went out of her way to ensure that parents felt safe, cared for and valued in the school setting. In *The Nursery School* (1919) she explains how she installed covered walkways from the nursery to home, so the parents were protected in bad weather. In addition to this, McMillan saw the education of parents as of equal significance. Her schools were open and there to influence and educate parents in the care of their children. To support this view fully she wrote books for parents, and later became involved as a lecturer with the Workers' Educational Association (WEA) in London. Steedman (1990) argues that McMillan saw the WEA as a useful platform for promoting the idea of the school clinic to a wide audience. Her school continues to this day, albeit in new premises, in Deptford.

Influences and links with other pioneers

McMillan carried forward from Pestalozzi and Froebel a child-centred holistic approach to learning based on play, movement and sensory experiences. Each child was considered of equal importance to the educator. Although play is seen to be central to provision in the EYFS I would question current understandings of what is meant by terms such as 'free play' and in particular 'child-initiated' and 'adult-led' activities. Early years training at present tends to focus on preparing students and teachers for delivering the curriculum, particularly in numeracy and literacy. Little training is offered about the nature of play inside or outside, free or guided. Our outcome-driven curriculum continues to contribute to these misunderstandings. There is little doubt that more needs to be done to develop a pedagogy which clarifies these issues and relates research to practice.

Froebel's garden assumes a mystical form with children waiting for their inner nature to unfold as they interact with nature. Nature is seen as the great healer in the midst of disease and squalor. The environment mattered to all the pioneers, in that it provided a secure, safe, loving base from which to grow. While Froebel's garden may have been criticized for being too far removed from the reality of children's lives, McMillan placed her garden at the centre of the slum world that she wanted to improve. In her view, the garden itself became an important factor in the reform of poverty. Nature was represented in the garden in the form of order in the face of chaos. The boundaries protected health from the threat of the slums. The garden was set out like a small community, where each age group had its own shelter and outdoor space. This included equipment relevant to the needs of the group such as small steps for the toddlers to climb. This is reminiscent of the equipment in the *I Ur och Skur* schools in Sweden, which featured rope swings in trees set at different heights to accommodate all abilities, from toddlers through to 6-year-olds (Joyce 2006). This will be discussed in the following chapter.

McMillan took Pestalozzi's and Froebel's outdoor occupations and changed them to suit the needs of her children. They became less didactic and more connected with the daily needs of the school community. Each activity was seen as a cognitive experience where children learn by doing: 'In every out-door Nursery there is work to be done. Certain morning tasks are given to everyone . . . feeding the rabbits, and birds, dusting, watering, and the arranging of flowers – clear litter which spoils the order of the place' (McMillan 1919: 89). Following Froebel and Pestalozzi she explored the local and wider environment with the children, visiting parks, museums, galleries, historic buildings and zoos. She saw this knowledge of the wider world as an essential part of their education and an important key to raising self-esteem and self-worth. Everything she showed them was to be available to everyone, including the poor. Lowndes (1960) claims that she told children, 'You may be poor now but if you want there is nothing to stop you sitting in the Houses of Parliament' (p. 72). There is little doubt that she had her friend Keir Hardie in mind when she said this. This legacy of excursions continues to be seen as an important part of provision today. However, it is so fraught with difficulties surrounding risk in our current legislative culture that many schools and practitioners decide against such trips to avoid possible prosecutions. The risk assessment paperwork alone is often enough to deter people. The loss for children incurred by our current regulatory craze is, of course, immense.

McMillan took from Pestalozzi and Froebel the view that people who work with young children have to be highly trained. This they saw as a prerequisite to quality care. She focused her training on the slum community where the children lived. Trainee teachers had to live in the community and complete one year of practical work before they started their academic study. This approach was strongly in line with that of Pestalozzi and Frohm who also advocated practice before theory. She was not satisfied with the contemporary, sentimental ideas about early childhood education which suggested that any nice girl would do for a nursery teacher, and that training was seen as unnecessary (McMillan 1919). She was not alone in this view. The early part of the century saw a rapid decline in the pupil–teacher system, which came under attack as an inefficient method of delivering mass education. Teachers at this time had low status and were poorly paid. After the First World War there was a great shortage, causing the government to take decisive action. Lloyd George enlisted the services of H.A.L. Fisher, the Oxford historian, to create an educational plan for the nation (Curtis 1948). Fisher understood that low pay and status would not attract the right kind of people to a profession central to the future health, well-being and prosperity of the nation. He established the Superannuation Act of 1918, which included all teachers. Pensions for teachers had originally been set up by Kay-Shuttleworth in the nineteenth century but had been withdrawn when the Revised Code of 1862 came into force. Teachers had become politicized by this time and the National Union of Teachers was formed. The Burnham Committee considered pay scales, which finally brought teachers in line with other professions in 1919.

The idea that young children do not need well-qualified teachers is still strong today. Choosing to work with younger pre-school children is often seen as taking a backward step, a demotion, and is also seen as 'women's work'. To her chagrin, McMillan experienced at first hand the impact of untrained help on practice during wartime. The government's strategy currently is to have a trained teacher in every nursery in the UK, including the private, independent, maintained and voluntary sectors. This has not been without its difficulties, especially in the current recession. It will be interesting to see if this level of provision is sustainable.

Also, as Montessori asserted, being outside is not enough in itself for young children. Practitioners need to be trained for an outdoor environment, which requires a different approach altogether, with different teaching and learning strategies. There is light on the horizon, however, in the shape of the growing number of Nature Schools and the Forest School Movement. These have developed their own pedagogy, as will be seen in Chapter 8. Education departments need to start looking outside the restrictive box of research on literacy and numeracy league tables and consider the urgent need for more appropriate training for teachers if the level of professionalism envisaged by Fisher is to be sustained. The legacy of Comenius, Pestalozzi, Froebel and McMillan has to be the true recognition of the early years as a discrete stage of learning. The EYFS is testament to this today, even if it is over-prescriptive in its present form.

I will now move on to explore the life and work of Gösta Frohm in Sweden and consider the influences which impacted on his ideas.

Reflective questions

Consider the following questions individually or in a groups:

- What were the main influences on McMillan's formation?
- What were her most important achievements and why?

7 Born to learn in nature: Gösta Frohm in Sweden (1908–99)

Figure 7.1   Gösta Frohm in 1997

Education and society in the time of Frohm

Before moving on to look at Gösta Frohm, a brief discussion of terms and an introduction to those interviewed for this study seems important. *Skogsmulle* is a fictional character created by Frohm to facilitate teaching young children about nature. It is also a foundation whose aim is to promote and protect

Frohm's ideas. As indicated in the Introduction, due to the lack of published data for this research, interviews were conducted with the president of the foundation, Jill Westermark, as well as members of *Friluftsfrämjandet*, the organization for which Frohm worked. These included Secretary General Bo Sköld, Helena Graffman and Harriet Guter, the member of the board responsible for *I Ur och Skur* (rain or shine). This is a developed pedagogy, which means a programme of educational theory and methodology in practice that follows on from Frohm's work with *Skogsmulle*. Magnus and Siw Linde are active members of the local branch of *Friluftsfrämjandet*. Interviews were also conducted with Frohm's daughters, Anna Frohm and Eva Josefsson, and his son Sten Frohm.

Gösta Frohm made an important contribution to thinking about teaching ecological concepts to young children, both in his native country of Sweden and internationally. What is interesting is that he was neither a philosopher nor an educationalist. His own education ended aged 19. He was a military man who taught skiing. So where did his vision for young children come from? To understand this phenomenon it is necessary to look at Frohm in his historical context. Sweden is a country which, from the eighteenth century, has depended on agriculture, mining and forestry. It has a long history of caring for nature, forests, rivers, lakes and the sea. Swedish people also have an established entitlement of access to nature and private land (*allemansrätten*), which is also highly significant.

The rise of Parliamentary democracy in Sweden in the nineteenth century promoted the idea that each person could become empowered to learn and participate in the democratic process (Læesøe and Öhman 2010). The evidence for this can be seen in Sweden's long tradition of adult education, largely supported by the philanthropy of non-conformist churches, temperance movements and trade unions (Boucher 1982). The best known of these is the Folk High School Movement, which was founded in Denmark by Frederik Severin Grundtvig (1783–1872) and came to Sweden in 1868 (Canfield 1965). This was similar in approach to that of Paulo Freire's (1921–97) philosophy of education, which was based on his idea of the pedagogy of the oppressed. He believed that people should be educated to be morally, intellectually and politically active so that they could bring about social change. Freire placed a strong emphasis on the reciprocal nature of teaching and learning, with the teacher learning from the child and the child learning from the teacher in an active participative way. This democratic approach to teaching and learning is central to current educational provision and policy in Sweden and has been integral to *Skogsmulle* and *I Ur och Skur* pedagogy and practice.

Industrialization and urbanization occurred later in Sweden than in the UK. The Social Democrats had been in power from 1934 to 1976 and had become a welfare state. They had also become associated with urbanization, industrialization and high taxes (OECD 1981). Linde (2010a) tells us that Frohm at this time was a leading member of *Friluftsfrämjandet*, a voluntary, apolitical, non-profit, independent organization which was founded in 1892. The organization had no religious affiliation. It had a close relationship to the military and promoted skiing activities for adults. Bo Sköld (2010), Secretary General of *Friluftsfrämjandet*, explained in interview that, gradually, other activities were added for younger people as well. They began to ski with the organization, the military helping with these activities. The children began by carving their own skis out of wood in school. From the 1920s *Friluftsfrämjandet* took children on trips to the mountains. After the First World War in Sweden, just as in England during Margaret McMillan's time, though for different reasons, there was great concern regarding the health of the nation. This resulted in government-sponsored outdoor activity to learn to ski and to improve physical well-being. Sköld mentioned that for two consecutive winters in the early 1950s there was very little snow for skiing and the instructors at *Friluftsfrämjandet* had to consider alternative activities for the children. This presented the perfect opportunity for Frohm to develop his ideas for children's outdoor activities.

Increasingly, Frohm felt that younger children were becoming more and more distanced from nature. To redress this he set up a *Skogsmulle* school for children from 5 to 6 years of age. Like McMillan and Froebel before him, he believed that his method of first-hand sensory experiences, which included regular visits to the forest, would compensate children for the strictures of modern-day living by reconnecting them with nature. His approach differed, however, in that he executed this through an imaginary character called *Skogsmulle*. (In Swedish *skog* means forest and *Mulle* is the name of a character who lives in the forest; Linde 2010a.) His youngest daughter Anna noted in an interview, 'He would have wanted all children to go to *Skogsmulle* because that's what [he felt] they need[ed] for their own personality, own needs. He wanted to create happier people' (2010a). Jill Westermark, an early childhood educator at Stockholm University and President of the *Skogsmulle* Foundation (Gösta Frohm's *Skogsmullestiftelse)*, saw the potential for similar, imaginative outdoor activities with children under 5 years of age but felt the *Mulle* character was too frightening for them. She formed a group in 1984 called *Skogsknytte* (which means ladybirds), which introduced the younger children to *Skogsmulle* ideas through play in nature. This group, alongside *Skogsmulle* and his friends, is now integral to her early years training courses at Stockholm University. The *Skogsmulle* Foundation itself was founded in 1988.

The introduction of the character of *Skogsmulle* in 1957 happened at a time when sweeping governmental changes, employing a more rationalist approach to educational reform, were taking place in Sweden (Boucher 1982). In their 1981 review of educational reforms in Sweden the OECD noted that in the 1940s, '. . . by European standards, Sweden had a weak and backward school system' (OECD 1981: 25). However, by 1975 the monarchy in Sweden was purely constitutional and the one-chamber Parliament (*Riksdag*) was formed by proportional representation every three years. The country has historically had a democratic and egalitarian character and the report adds that by the 1980s the government had created 'an explicitly egalitarian and unified system of education' (p. 19). Democracy and its concomitant qualities of co-operation and consensus became a central feature of Swedish education. A consequence of this after 1976 was devolved spending to municipalities, which nonetheless continued to work within national policies. This allowed for more flexibility to meet educational demands at local level, as well as greater opportunities for experimentation and innovatory practice.

However, older views still held sway. The work of Ellen Karolina Sofia Key (1849–1926), a controversial, self-taught feminist writer at the turn of the century, was still influential around the time when *Skogsmulle* appeared. She was a Folk High School teacher and an ardent, lifelong admirer of Henrik Ibsen (1828–1906), the nineteenth-century Norwegian playwright, poet and theatre director. It is likely that Ibsen influenced Key's position on challenging traditional assumptions, particularly regarding morality issues. Like Margaret McMillan, she was a liberal reformer who wanted to promote the needs of working people. Her seminal work *The Century of the Child* was translated into English in 1909. It was originally published in Swedish in 1900, expounding the history of education, its moral failings and the role it should take in the future (Kent 2008). This work, in Kent's view, represented a major shift in thinking about children as individuals, their well-being, and their educational needs as civic beings. In her biography of Key, Nyström (1913) explains how women's hard-earned equality in the workplace was, in Key's view, misplaced since she believed that, rather than imitating men, women should be embracing their capacity to be excellent mothers. She believed that the home ought to be the centre for children's education in the early years. In the following extract Key expounds her views on education at the turn of the century by scathingly describing a teaching approach which Frohm himself would probably have experienced as a child. '. . . a cramming system . . . where the mental food is accepted from the teacher instead of the pupil being obliged to overcome his own difficulties and crack the nuts of knowledge with his own teeth' (Nyström 1913: 78). Like Key, Frohm did not see the child as a passive recipient of knowledge. He wanted children to have a questioning, hands-on, sensory experience of the world. Westermark remarked that Key's ideas have been central to Swedish thinking on current early childhood education and to the *Skogsmulle* concept in particular. Key's emphasis on individualism and a love of the outdoors, as well as her passionate interest in nature, added greatly to her influence on Frohm. The importance of the family, and the critical role of the mother as central to this, she shares with Comenius and all the pioneers considered in this book. Frohm himself informs us, in a short video of his life entitled *En Smula Gösta* (A Little Bit of Gösta), that it was his own mother who inspired his love and interest in nature (Hedlund 1997).

Frohm had been married and divorced twice and had four children: three daughters and a son. His two children from his first marriage were Eva (1937–present) and Gun (1933–present). His two children from his second marriage were Sten (1963–present) and Anna (1961–present). Anna believed that her father modelled his *Skogsmulle* ideas on what he did with his own children. Anna and Sten spent their early years leading an active outdoor life while living at Lida near Stockholm with their mother and father. 'We were like guinea pigs for him . . . I knew all the flowers when I was 3. All the way down to the lake he was testing. He wanted us to have a lot of knowledge about nature and how to live the life . . . he was a demanding father' (Frohm 2010a).

She continued by saying that in order to entice his own children to go on trips with him he would prepare an album of photographs and maps of the place he intended to visit and present this with so much enthusiasm that it was difficult to resist. Anna also noted that her father read a great deal and knew about other pedagogues such as Froebel and Montessori. However, she explains how he learned about Steiner the hard way. When she strongly resisted his ideas, in a bid to assert her own individuality by sending her first child to a Steiner school rather than to the *I Ur och Skur* Mulleborg, he did not speak to her for three months. He could not believe that she would expose her child to a teaching approach which did not, in his view, welcome close child and parent interaction at school. Parental involvement and close interaction between children, parents and teachers were central to Frohm's philosophy and practice.

The early life and development of Frohm

Frohm was born in Sollefteå in Northern Sweden in 1908. He had one sister. His oldest daughter Eva explained in a telephone communication in August 2010 that her grandmother, Frohm's mother, was a harsh, disciplined woman, a farmer's daughter from a respectable, local middle-class family. His father was a Walloon who worked on the Swedish railways as a navvy. Frohm was very proud of this heritage (Josefsson 2010). The Walloons started migrating from Wallonia, now Belgium, from as early as the 1620s to work in the iron foundries in northern Sweden. They were originally led by Louis de Geer (1587–1652). He was a wealthy industrialist and arms manufacturer whose son

Laurens had in fact been an important patron of Comenius in the seventeenth century (Kent 2008).

Frohm went to the local elementary and high schools. His family were Swedish Lutherans and Frohm often told his children how his mother had wanted him to become a priest. She even collected furniture for him to use later in that role. He studied theology for a time at Uppsala University but left because of the heavy drinking he witnessed among his classmates (Josefsson 2010). Frohm states clearly in *En Smula Gösta* (A Little Bit of Gösta) that he was far too emotional a character to become a priest and freely admitted that his feelings were so strong that he always cried at weddings and funerals. His daughter Anna corroborated this, adding that 'when he read the newspaper his tears were on the page'. Although religion was a central feature of his upbringing it was only later in life that it became of real significance to him. Anna recalled how disappointed he was when she did not make her confirmation. She added that 'the church was important for him in the matter of moral things and ethics' (Frohm 2010a).

He left the Gymnasium aged 18. This was the name given to the old state grammar schools which had, since the time of Gustavus Adolphus (1594–1632), always been open to boys of all social classes and, from 1927, to girls as well (Düring 1951). From there he was conscripted into the army for two years. Since jobs were scarce in Sweden and elsewhere in Europe at this time of massive unemployment, he was persuaded in 1928 to pursue a career in the army. He got a job in Stockholm at the military headquarters, where he became a Physical Training Officer. In this role, according to his son Sten, he was a skiing instructor but was also involved in practical survival studies with researchers and doctors, such as building igloos and sleeping in the snow. His daughter Anna adds in interview that he also taught dancing while in the army. Sköld explains how the conscripts in the military combined the theoretical side of their training with their practice in the outdoors. They generally learned by *doing*, using their senses to problem solve as they worked together co-operatively in groups. This training approach of 'learning by doing' was later to significantly influence Frohm in his development of the *Skogsmulle* concept. His military experience also put a premium on the use of the outdoors in education. This outdoor life suited him since 'he was very much a nature person' (Josefsson 2010). This enthusiasm continued into old age when, aged 80, he still went on hiking and camping trips with his daughter Anna (Frohm 2010a). Frohm came from an age when communication itself was more direct and manual than in the present. He preferred to write most of his communications by hand, in capital letters, always carrying a pencil for this purpose and a knife to sharpen it. An example of a handwritten communication from Frohm is shown in Figure 7.2.

In 1946 Frohm was recruited by *Friluftsfrämjandet* and moved to Stockholm. He stayed with the organization until he retired in 1973.

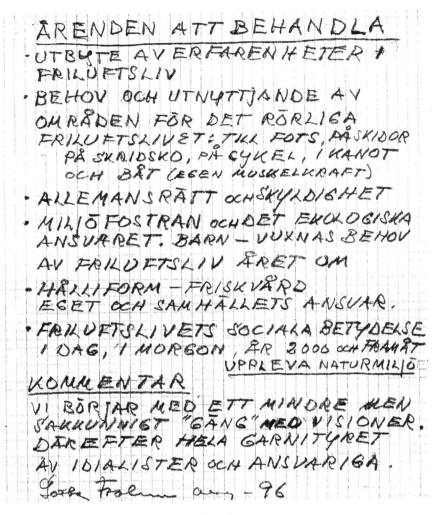

Figure 7.2 Handwritten communication from Frohm

Implication of his ideas in practice

Frohm believed that in order to develop a love and respect for nature it is important to start with young children before they become corrupted by the lure of society, technology and commercialism (Frohm 2010b). In the 1950s when Frohm started his open-air *Skogsmulle* School, most mothers were at home rearing their children and there was little or no childcare as we know it today. Linde (2010a) explains how the idea became very popular and many of the mothers, who were predominantly middle class, trained to become *Skogsmulle* leaders themselves. The *Skogsmulle* philosophy was based on the simple premise that 'if you can help children to love nature, they will take care of nature because you cherish things you love' (p. 1). This approach involved the fictional figure of *Skogsmulle* who helps children to 'love nature through fairy tales, songs and games while out in the woods studying plants and animals' (p. 1). In the beginning all *Skogsmulle* schools were run by volunteers from *Friluftsfrämjandet*. They met once a week for about three hours, always outdoors in the forest, for a total of 15–20 hours. This was done in spring and autumn. Frohm's daughter Eva explained how her father became 'Mr *Friluftsfrämjandet*' when she was a young child, as he travelled the country promoting the *Skogsmulle* concept (Josefsson 2010). He built up local networks of volunteers and trained them. She described him as a good organizer and leader but one who wanted to be in complete control of the interpretation of his ideas by other individuals and groups.

Frohm recognized that people were different and required different tools to deliver his message. He wrote story books to facilitate this process. Derry (1979) explains that folktales derived from old Scandinavian legends play a central part in Swedish culture. The first book, *Skogsmulle* (1970), introduced his main character and includes the story of how he was born in the forest. Other books followed telling the story of *Skogsmulle's* three friends. *Skogsmulle och Fjällfina* (1971) teaches the children how to look after high ground such as hills and mountains; *Laxe* (1978) teaches children how to look after the water in our rivers and seas and *Nova* (1997), who comes from a totally unpolluted planet, teaches us how to look after our own (Linde 2010a). These books, jointly published by a Stockholm publisher and *Friluftsfrämjandet*, were used by trained leaders but have subsequently been replaced by other teaching means.

Frohm created a fifth character called *Urban*, who was designed to teach the children how to deal with contemporary issues associated with urbaniza-tion and industrialization such as litter, vandalism and graffiti. At that time the *Skogsmulle* Foundation thought the character too negative and did not support its use. There are, however, plans in the Foundation to resurrect this character in the near future (Westermark 2010). In Sollefteå, Lida and Sunnersta, which is just outside Uppsala, *Friluftsfrämjandet* has set up trails through the forest to help visiting children explore their immediate environment through the senses of *Mulle, Laxe, Fjällfina* and *Nova*. Even though Frohm's old books are no longer in use, the characters are still very much in evidence. Each trail ends with a shelter representing one of their homes (see Figure 7.3). Leaders frequently dress up as these characters or use puppets to greet the children when they visit and to engage them in the exploration of nature (Robertson 2008).

Figure 7.3 Anna Frohm aged 9 outside *Fjällfina*'s house in Sollefteå

In addition to story books, Frohm also employed music as a teaching and learning strategy (see Figure 7.4). He was an accomplished musician who played the ukulele, piano, guitar, the harmonica and accordion. He loved to perform and his daughter Eva added that he was a good singer too. 'It was never dull when Gösta Frohm was around' (Josefsson 2010). He composed

Figure 7.4   Gösta Frohm singing and playing the accordion with children at Mulleborg, 1990

songs about all the characters and even wrote a children's opera in the 1980s on an environmental protection theme, when he co-operated with a professional musician, Jan-Åke Hillerud (1938–present). In an obituary in the *Svenska Dagbladet*, the Swedish national daily newspaper, Frohm's friend Omar Magnergard notes that music was central to Frohm's life (Magnergard 1999). Helena Graffman from *Friluftsfrämjandet* (Graffman 2010) remarked that all her discussions with Frohm happened seated at the piano beside him.

The OECD shows that by 1981 most children in Sweden aged 6 years of age received some pre-school education to prepare them for compulsory education. However, even at this stage there was little or no state provision for children below that age, with the exception of children with special needs and this came under the 'welfare' umbrella. The report argues that this welfare umbrella may have been advantageous to the Swedish pre-school in that it allowed them greater independence and freedom to increase their flexibility than if they had been part of the national educational system. When deregulation came into force in 1985 this was an optimum time for experimentation and a good time for parents to think about opening their own *I Ur och Skur* pedagogic pre-school. This was in advance of a government initiative in 1987 when, for the first time, government pedagogic recommendations for pre-school were made. These were not statutory and could be interpreted at local level depending on needs. When the *Skogsmulle* concept later came to be used in kindergartens, nurseries and pre-schools, the condition was that its pedagogues should attend a *Skogsmulle* leader course held by *Friluftsfrämjandet*. They were then entitled to use *Skogsmulle* activities, either in their gardens or nearby forest.

A significant ideological shift occurred in educational policy and practice in the early 1990s in Sweden when a right-wing political majority in Parliament led to a rapid spread of the free market, as it did in the UK at the same time (Johansson 1997). The pre-school in Sweden now became part of the educational rather than welfare system of governance and acquired its own curriculum in 1998. This, however, differed from the UK in that national guidelines were administered and followed at a local level, a democratic strategy designed by government to allow for greater child, parent and teacher participation. Another significant difference from the UK equivalent curriculum is that there were no goals to be 'reached' in the Swedish curriculum, only goals to be 'strived towards' (Roth and Månsson 2009: 179), something explicitly aimed at developing a democratic citizen (Alvestad and Samuelsson 1999). This new curriculum has not only raised the profile of children from 1 to 5 years of age but it has also created a 'new professionalism' among teachers which involves monitoring, evaluation and availability for 'public inspection and control' (Löfdahl and Prieto 2009: 262). This accountability focus brings the pre-school into competition with others in their bid to secure parents and children. The same issue has been prominent in the UK since the 1990s. With these changes funding became, in Johansson's words, 'attached to the product', and the pre-school received a fixed amount for each child (1997: 34). However, it must be noted that the Swedish 'product' does not mean the same as in market-dominated UK.

Moss (2009) suggests alternatives to this market-led approach, showcasing the Reggio Emilia democratic experimentalism pedagogy. This political approach to learning was a collective response to a new identity in the northern Italian town of Reggio Emilia at the end of the Second World War, after years of Fascist oppression. Women who had been involved in the Resistance Movement (the Unite Italian Women, or UDI) fought to develop pre-schools for their children. They wanted schools that would encourage their children to think for themselves. They invited the educationalist Loris Malaguzzi (1920–94), who was then a teacher, to co-ordinate the educational projects at these schools and develop a long-term view of possibilities for education. Fundamental to this approach are their close links with the city and the view that the child is strong, competent and rich in potential. Westermark (2010) argues that Swedish pre-school already held this democratic, creative philosophy and the introduction of the Reggio presence in Sweden has, in her view, influenced pre-schools, 'not for the children but for politics'. The prominence of documentation in the Swedish model clearly echoes the same emphasis in the Reggio approach.

Frohm's legacy: the *Skogsmulle/I Ur och Skur* concept

The *Skogsmulle* concept is remembered by many. Robertson (2008) informs us that one out of every four Swedish people has experienced *Skogsmulle* activities. *Friluftsfrämjandet* noted (17 June 2010) that even Crown Princess Victoria, Protectress of their organization's children's activities, enjoyed *Skogsmulle* School as a child. Frohm's son Sten (Frohm 2010b) noted that it was his father's dream to get just one *Mulle*-educated child into government so as to have an impact on the wider world. Frohm's dream has in fact come true. Anders Borg has been the Minister of Finance in the government (*Regeringen*) since 2006. He was a *Mulle* child whose own children went to *I Ur och Skur* in Lidingö, near Stockholm. Borg, in fact, helped to run the pre-school as part of the parents' group. Sten Frohm described his father as an early environmentalist who cared deeply about the world's natural resources. In 1997 the government recognized his commitment to children and nature and presented him with the 'Illis Quorum' medal (*Skogsmulle* Foundation 1999). This is the highest award that can be given to any person by the Swedish government.

Frohm's biggest legacy, in my view, is the evolution of the *I Ur och Skur*. Siw Linde a pharmacist, trained *Skogsmulle* leader and pre-school teacher, took the *Skogsmulle* concept and, to use Anna Frohm's words, 'helped [Frohm] to structure his passion' (2010a). Along with another teacher, Susanne Drougge, Linde set up her own school at Mulleborg, strongly supported by her husband Magnus and the local community (Linde 2010b). Linde took Frohm's practice-led, imaginative approach, while appreciating his view that 'you [first] have to have it here in the heart and then you have it in the brain' (Frohm 2010a). To this first-hand, sensory approach to learning outdoors through nature she, however, was careful to add the method and theory. This involved looking more closely at the potential for intellectual, physical, emotional and social development in the outdoor environment, adult–child interaction, parental involvement and engagement with the wider community. However, it took *Friluftsfrämjandet* several years to see how important a development this was and to offer their full support (Linde 2010b).

Pre-school provision in Sweden at this time was Froebelian-based and underpinned by the theory and practice of Rousseau and Pestalozzi, which was later developed by Key and Dewey at the beginning of the twentieth century. Children played outside in gardens and went out on trips but no one at this time was taking children into the natural world as a regular part of provision.

This was a new departure, as was the theory and methodology that grew up alongside this practice. Central to *I Ur och Skur* thinking is reflexive practice where adults and children reflect on their experiences and learn from them, including seeing things through children's eyes. Adults and children learn together in nature in a Vygotskian way, with the adults 'scaffolding' children's learning and moving them on to the next stage. This is done through close observation and active listening as well as close interaction between adults and children. Graffman (2010) and Guter (2010) described how this method is based on teaching, observing, experiencing and acting *together with* the children. Before the 1998 curriculum, children in mainstream provision were given all the answers just as they were at the beginning of the twentieth century in Key's time. Post-1998 the teacher does not give all the answers. The children are taught to be curious and find the answers together with the teacher. This new curriculum promotes equality and one of the goals, for example, is to work towards gender equality by giving each child the chance to develop into a unique individual. The unique child in the DfES (2007a) EYFS in the UK immediately comes to mind but without the Swedish political emphasis on the underpinning qualities of democracy and equality. Figure 7.5 clearly illustrates the philosophy of *I Ur och Skur* as outlined in their mission statement, with its strong leaning towards education for sustainability and

Figure 7.5 *I Ur och Skur* mission statement

cognitive understanding of children's learning. It is clear that this vision starts with valuing the individual and then moves towards learning how to work co-operatively in groups. It therefore works towards becoming a responsible citizen and, finally, to playing an active, informed part in considering global environmental issues.

There are now approximately two hundred and twenty-three *I Ur och Skur* units all over Sweden, catering for children from 1 to 11 years of age. This figure includes 16 outdoor primary schools, the first one of which was called *Utsikten* (which means 'the view'). Despite the fact that this movement has grown so much in popularity, its pedagogy is still relatively little known in Sweden, in much the same way as the Reggio approach is little known in Italy. Practitioners like myself from the UK, Germany, Finland, Russia, Latvia and Japan have visited Sweden and, inspired by the good practice, have implemented much of the pedagogy on returning to our own countries (see Figure 7.6).

The reasons for this lack of awareness of *I Ur och Skur* are interesting. (It should be remembered, however, how popular the *Skogsmulle* approach has been.) Sköld (2010) mentions that on a recent visit to Sweden a group of Japanese pedagogues questioned the Minister of Education regarding *I Ur och Skur*. The minister was unfamiliar with the group or its popularity.

Figure 7.6   The author's first view of an *I Ur och Skur* pre-school

Sköld believes, however, that this international interest and growing popularity abroad gives the pedagogy of *I Ur och Skur* and *Skogsmulle* a national credibility, which is likely to encourage a further spread of these ideas in Sweden. A longer term reason for the low profile of *I Ur och Skur* is the place of the *Jante Law*, a concept formulated by a Danish man called Aksel Sandemose (1899–1965) in a novel entitled *En flyktning krysser sitt spor* (1933) (A Fugitive Crosses the Tracks). This unofficial 'law', it is claimed, has been adopted by many Swedes. Everybody knows about it but nobody talks about it. In their view it inhibits academic research studies on the efficacy of their approach to learning. Its impact seems to be based on national democratic understandings of equality where there appears to exist a conflict between equality and individualism. Linde talked about being taught as a child always to praise others' achievements and never to put herself above anyone else. This, coupled with the Swedish maxim for good living, *Lagom*, a Swedish word which roughly translates as 'everything in moderation', describes the limited view of the individual in Swedish society (Graffman 2010; Guter 2010; Sköld 2010). The OECD describes this paradox in the following way: 'One of the drawbacks of a drive to treat everybody equally is that there is so strong a concern with global outcomes "for everybody", that the school, the teacher and the pupil's right to be treated differentially is resisted' (1981: 39).

Sköld went on to say that the time had come for *I Ur och Skur* to move on, put aside these restrictions and promote themselves in the interests of children and in their own interest within such a competitive market. *I Ur och Skur* has begun to market their ideals and have found it necessary to document their approach, more in line with the UK's model, so that they can be sustainable. Their contribution to the pedagogy of outdoor learning was rewarded in 2009 by winning the Nordic Council Nature and Environment Prize (Norden 2009). The Adjudicating Committee's comments echo my own perceptions and appreciation of this approach to teaching and learning:

> *I Ur och Skur* serves as a model to emulate, illustrating perfectly how time spent in the great outdoors enhances a child's wellbeing . . . [its] purpose . . . is to promote the development of the child through linking outdoor activities to learning . . . all of the activities provide the children with a better understanding of nature.
>
> (Norden 2009: 1)

The following images are examples of young children enjoying the *Skogsmulle/I Ur och Skur* experience around the world in Latvia (Figure 7.6), Japan (Figure 7.7) and Russia (Figure 7.8). (All photographs are courtesy of Magnus Linde.)

Figure 7.7   Children in Latvia visiting *Mulle* (Siw Linde) in the forest

Figure 7.8   Children in Ichijima, Japan, exploring their environment

Figure 7.9   Russian children greet *Mulle*

In the next chapter I will explore how Forest Schools have developed in the UK.

Reflective questions

Consider the following questions individually or in a group:

- What was Frohm's understanding of nature? How did this influence his practice?
- Frohm: a visionary or a pedagogue?

8 Born to be free: Forest Schools in the UK (1950s–present)

Education and society in the time of Forest Schools

Before embarking on an exploration of Forest Schools, it is necessary to consider the question of pedagogy in the UK and what is meant by this from the 1950s to the present day. There has been much debate since the 1980s about whether or not pedagogy, in the sense of theory of education, exists in the UK. Brian Simon first raised the question in 1981, 'Why no pedagogy in England?' (Simon 1981). He defined pedagogy as 'a science of teaching embodying both curriculum and methodology', and suggested that a historical perspective was essential to understanding the absence of this phenomenon (p. 125). Simon deliberated as to why this idea was so alien to our experience. The concept of pedagogy was, he argued, held in high esteem on the Continent. There it was seen to originate from Comenius in the seventeenth century and then developed in the nineteenth century by Pestalozzi, Herbart, Froebel and others. Simon concluded that teaching, as a profession and serious subject of study, was denigrated historically by the public schools and ancient universities of England. Oxford, for example, was still without a Chair of Education in 1981. Consequently, in his view, few resources were allocated to this area and little serious experimental or scholarly studies were undertaken which might have led to a pedagogy. Alexander took up the same argument in 2004 and it continues to the present day. Stephen (2010) again questions the absence of any systematic pedagogy in practice or policy making, despite the growth in research evidence regarding teaching and how children learn. In this longitudinal study Stephen cites Siraj-Blatchford, who describes practitioners as 'recoiling' at the term pedagogy. She argues that although they associate the term with teaching, they have no real engagement in pedagogical discourse or thinking as a basis for practice development. It is in this context – as opposed to the concept of pedagogy as a science, which is strongly rooted in the tradition of education in the Swedish example – that we can now begin to explore the development of Forest Schools in the UK.

A significant shift in thinking occurred in the 1990s when UK interest in pedagogy took the form of an in-depth exploration of the Swedish model. According to Bond (2005: 1), 'the current manifestation of Forest Schools originated in Sweden in the 1950s, as a way of helping youngsters to learn about the natural world through stories, songs and practical experiences'. This approach was strongly embedded in a long Swedish tradition of systematic thought and research about understanding the pedagogy. Knight (2009) agrees and adds that by the 1980s Forest Schools were well established in most Scandinavian countries and became central to early years provision in Denmark and Sweden. The Forest Education Initiative (FEI) (2009) argues that this approach was used as far back as the early 1920s in the UK as a strategy for teaching children about the natural world. There is little evidence, however, to substantiate this claim. Forest Schools were first introduced to the UK in the 1990s, at the height of curriculum reform, as a possible counter to the newly introduced rigid and prescriptive National Curriculum. A group of lecturers and trainee nursery nurses from Bridgwater College in Somerset visited Denmark in 1993 and brought the concept back with them. The child-centred core element of this approach to learning, which they observed, warrants some investigation historically. It has been central to educational thinking since the 1950s in the UK and, according to Maynard (2007b), 'reached the peak of official acceptance in the late 1960s' (p. 380). Although the aftermath of the Second World War brought peace, it also brought a fall in the population, which was accompanied by deterioration in economic performance in the face of international competition (Taylor 1981). Nurseries for young children closed when the war ended and women were no longer needed in the workforce. With the exception of those children in the most deprived areas, no provision was made for children under 5, despite promises made in the 1944 Education Act. The Ministry of Education went further, banning the expansion of nurseries in Education Circular 8/60, so that funds could be redirected at raising the school age and reducing class sizes (Kwon 2002).

The question remains, how could a pedagogy develop when there was no state provision for the under-5s? Just as the mothers at home after the war in Reggio Emilia and Sweden began to create play settings for their own children in the absence of adequate state provision, so too did the mothers in the UK. Belle Tutaev, a young mother living in London, is credited with the founding of the playgroup movement in 1961. Along with a neighbour, she organized a nursery group in a church hall to cater for the needs of her 4-year-old (Pre-School Learning Alliance 2010). This was how the Pre-School Playgroups Association came into being. It was widely accepted by the government as a low-cost substitute for nursery schools. The movement grew in popularity and in its heyday reached a membership of 20,000. Its approach was child-centred and focused on parental involvement, as did Reggio and *Skogsmulle*. According to Simon (1981: 140), this child-centred approach to learning had dominated educational thinking since the 1920s and reached its 'apotheosis' in the 1967 Plowden Report, which he describes as 'the pedagogic romanticism'. In his view, the report was a further blow to the development of education as a science involving something other than the needs of the individual, namely, an understanding of the general principles of teaching.

The outcomes of the Plowden Report (1967) were based on Jean Piaget's (1896–1980) developmentalist and 'readiness' concepts. Piaget's work was highly influential and widely accepted at this time. On the strength of this, Pound (2005) notes that Piaget's ideas have been adopted by many as the basis for good practice, despite the fact that his work has currently been the subject of much criticism. John Dewey's (1859–1952) views on an integrated, holistic early childhood curriculum as opposed to a subject-based curriculum opened a debate on free play (Kwon 2002). At the same time, individual psychology, social psychology and the newly popular discipline of sociology were developing. Each child came to be seen as unique and requiring its own individual pedagogy, a nightmare scenario for teachers working autonomously in a pragmatic, piecemeal way in a decentralized system with no overarching structure. This child-centred learning by discovery advocated by Plowden required little adult intervention. It was considered sufficient for the child to interact independently with an instructive environment. Kwon (2002) argues that the approach was deeply criticized by many as not being in the child's best interests. From my own perspective as a teacher at that time, the workload was not in the adult's interests either.

A political shift to the right from 1979 to 1997 brought a significant change in educational policy which was then taken further by Tony Blair's New Labour governments (1997–2007). This told teachers what to teach and how to teach it. Margaret Thatcher's hostility to the progressive trends of Plowden resulted in the 1988 Education Reform Act and the introduction of the National Curriculum. Although the child was still regarded as central to the learning process, he or she no longer had any control over what or how learning took place. The National Curriculum brought with it its own theories and methodologies of education but not the pedagogy envisaged by Simon and Alexander. With it instead came prescription, inspection, increased government intervention and decreased teacher autonomy. This teacher autonomy had been in evidence since the payment by results system in 1898 and the Elementary Code in 1926. It did, however, bring the long-awaited provision of nursery places for the under-5s, though the low-cost strategy of placing many 4-year-olds in reception classes caused much consternation and disapproval within and outside the teaching profession. This 1988 Reform Act also came with curriculum guidelines for the youngest children. These were later replaced in 2008 by a statutory curriculum for birth to 5-year-olds, the Early Years Foundation Stage. This documentation was accompanied by a highly regulated system of assessment, inspection and published league tables. Anning

(1998) argues that early childhood education then became a highly visible political issue used to attract votes and focusing totally on preparing children for school. Conservative policy exposed pre-school provision to market forces where settings, schools and providers were in direct competition with one another. A huge plus for the Plowden Report and the EYFS, however, is that both promoted outdoor learning as a viable environment for learning. Sadly, the debate regarding pedagogy and the outdoors remains relatively unexplored outside the Forest School experience. Such a debate is absolutely necessary for the future of outdoor learning and for early years education in general. Pedagogy, sustained critical thinking about practice, needs to be at the centre, not the periphery of education.

The early years and development of Forest Schools

Forest School is a Scandinavian approach to outdoor learning. As a consequence of the Bridgwater visit to Denmark, the group set up a Forest School for their own college children. They later extended this to include children with special needs and, eventually, students of all ages were given the opportunity to have this experience. They went on to develop accredited training courses through the Open College Network (OCN), and a Business and Technology Education Council (BTEC) qualification for Forest School leaders and practitioners. Sara Bond, in her 2007 conference paper at Anglia Ruskin University, explained how the Forest School Movement developed initially in the West Country, then in Wales and Oxfordshire. She adds that the Greenlight Trust, an environmental charity based in Suffolk and funded by the Forestry Education Initiative (FEI), led the development of Forest Schools in the East of England. There are now Forest Schools throughout England, Wales, Scotland and Northern Ireland. Forest School leaders include a wide range of people from very different backgrounds such as, for example, woodland owners, teachers, early years workers and craftspeople.

Bond (2007) discusses possible links between Forest School and other historical movements promoting outdoor learning. She cites McMillan's work in the early twentieth century with its emphasis on creating a healthier citizenry. It was in this spirit of supporting young people in their physical, mental and spiritual development that the Scouting Movement was founded in 1907 by Lord Baden-Powell (1857–1941), a national hero at the time. Like Frohm, Baden-Powell was a military man, a retired army general who served in South Africa and British India in the 1880s and 1890s (ScoutBaseUK 2010). The Scouting Movement clearly reflects these military experiences with its emphasis on outdoor activities. The Scouting accoutrements of the uniform and flag ceremonies encouraged military prowess and separate it completely from the Swedish *Skogsmulle* model. The Scouts were initially imperialistic and militaristic. The Girl Guides Movement was then created in 1910 with similar ends in view.

An offshoot of the Scouting Movement was another little-known movement founded in 1920 and called the Kindred of the Kibbo Kift (Elwell-Sutton n.d.). Its founder was 26-year-old John Hargrave, the son of an artist and Quaker, also an active member of Baden-Powell's Scouting Movement. He was expelled from the movement for questioning its principles and went on to set up his own group. Although Hargrave centred his seven-point covenant on outdoor educational activities for children he rejected Baden-Powell's militaristic approach. Like Frohm and Baden-Powell, however, his own development and ideas were strongly influenced by his own war experiences. He was a sergeant in the Gallipoli and Salonika campaigns. Elwell-Sutton notes that Hargrave's influence on the German youth movement of the twenties is fully acknowledged by many authorities. The policy of 'Social Credit', as part of its covenant, led to the politicization of the movement. This was an economic plan developed by a British engineer called Major C.H. Douglas (1879–1952), who believed in a form of economic democracy. In his view power should be in the hands of the individual rather than governments and big banks. He envisaged a future under a system where people could choose to work less and enjoy greater leisure.

However, the Kibbo Kift group eventually became militarized, holding public marches and demonstrations. They were known as the 'Greenshirts' because of the uniform they wore. The group disbanded in 1951. A surviving breakaway group from the Kibbo Kift, the Woodcraft Folk, celebrated its eightieth anniversary in 2007. *Skogsmulle* and Forest Schools are not like Kibbo Kift. They are not militaristic, nationalistic, paternalistic or political in these ways. They seriously teach young children how to be in the world, how to respect the environment and one another.

The Forest School philosophy is properly thought out and designed to enhance mainstream education and offer, in a professional manner, an alternative curriculum in an outdoor context. It is based on a desire to provide young children with an education that inspires appreciation of the natural world and, in so doing, encourage a responsible attitude to the natural world in later life. Much of the evidence to date regarding the efficacy of this approach is anecdotal, although there is a growing awareness of the need for further in-depth research. O'Brien and Murray (2007) indicate that although research has been done in this area it is often not available in English. The New Economics Foundation (Murray 2003) has, however, completed a thorough evaluation of a project in Wales, while Rickinson et al. (2004) include Forest Schools in their *Review of Research on Outdoor Learning*. Norfolk Schools are creating evaluative frameworks for practitioners to collect data for documenting pilot projects (Norfolk Schools 2010).

In her research-based report on the impact of outdoor learning on children's whole development from birth to 18, Malone (2008) praises the easily adapted assessment model created by UK Forest Schools. Many other providers across the UK are now seeing the importance of evidence-based research into Forest Schools and are joining in the documentation process. Malone urges practitioners to increase the evidence base in order to guide researchers better. This in turn will convince educators, parents and politicians of the important contribution an effective use of the outdoors can contribute to children's learning. Without research, she argues, 'The battle will continue to be between what is seen as core activities for children's education – the real work in the classroom and the additional "fun" work that goes on outside the classroom' (Malone 2008: 25). In other words, the battle is between those who believe in the indoor classroom as the place where learning really occurs and those who see this as a narrow and outmoded view which negates the opportunities that exist for learning outdoors.

Forest School is an important manifestation of contemporary outdoor learning. Its methods suit young people and children with special needs, while offering a flexible approach to learning within a range of learning styles. It recommends a high ratio of adults to children. This recommendation is backed by research in the Effective Provision of Pre-School Education (EPPE) Project (Sylva et al. 2004) as a clear indicator for success in the education of pre-school children. The benefits of this approach are said to include the particular attributes outlined in Table 8.1. It can clearly be seen how these benefits slot into the EYFS curriculum and the *Every Child Matters* agenda (DfES 2003b).

Implication of these ideas in my practice

A Forest School can be described in the following way: it employs a woodland setting or other outdoor area as a classroom, where groups of children with adult leaders spend a certain fixed proportion of their teaching time, normally half a day a week. The children build a shelter, learn to keep themselves safe and enjoy the chance to explore the environment. Knight (2009) argues, however, that there is a significant difference between the Scandinavian Forest

Table 8.1   Perceived benefits of this approach to learning

The Forest School approach to learning
• Development of social skills and team work • Development of physical skills • Development of communication skills • Development of knowledge and understanding of the environment • Increased self-confidence and self-belief • Increased motivation and concentration

School approach and that used in the UK. The main cultural difference, she suggests, is that the majority of Scandinavians use the countryside regularly whereas this is not the case in the UK. The Scandinavians are also a less industrialized and urbanized culture which has retained its closeness to nature. Their approach to outdoor learning is largely based on socialization and free play in the Froebelian sense. The UK approach has been adapted to accommodate the British attitude to the outdoors and to risk in particular. The Scandinavians have a strong tradition of the healthy body and an affinity with nature. This is not the case in the UK, especially more so now, where the outdoors is not part of everyday life. The British term 'inclement weather' says so much about UK thoughts regarding the outdoors. When it is cold or wet, you stay inside with the heating on. The Scandinavian maxim, which states that there is no such thing as bad weather, only bad clothing, does little to influence British attitudes. The UK has also had to accommodate a prescriptive early years curriculum, a feature notable by its absence in the Scandinavian setting. In her book, *Forest Schools and Outdoor Learning in the Early Years*, Knight (2009: 14) seeks to find a 'sustainable . . . shared national model' for UK Forest Schools. Table 8.2 shows a list of the structures which she has observed as integral to her experience of Forest Schools. She believes they are also generic to the ethos of this approach, as opposed to outdoor learning in general.

The Forest School approach to risk in the UK is carefully structured, working with appropriate reduced risk, rather than total elimination of all risk likely to lead to litigation. The children's safety is paramount but the role of

Table 8.2   Adaptation of Knight's interpretation of Forest Schools (2009: 15–17)

What makes Forest Schools different from outdoor learning in general?

- Forest School is not the usual setting. It happens in a wood, forest, space away from normal setting
- Forest School has its own rules, e.g. how close to sit to the fire, how to handle tools, sticks etc.
- Risk is managed, i.e. leaders do regular, rigorous risk assessments and identify risk and appropriate action. This does not mean that risk is always removed. It may be enough, for instance, to simply point the risk out to the children
- Forest School happens in six-week blocks i.e. children visit the site for half a day over a period of six weeks. Others argue, myself included, that ideally early years children should spend half a day a week over a period of one year
- Forest School happens in all weathers
- Forest School is based on trust
- The adult role is facilitative
- Sessions are play-based and child-led
- There is a strong structure to the sessions
- All the staff are Forest School trained

---

challenge as a learning tool is thoughtfully preserved. In his New Economic Foundation (NEF) *Forest School Evaluation Project*, Murray (2003) identified a similar list of ten critical success factors as generic to a thriving Forest School. These mirror Knight's list, with the addition of the following features:

- good access to the Forest School;
- familiar routines and structures to sessions;
- enjoyment by teachers and leaders;
- parent/carer involvement in Forest School activities.

Many would argue that the above lists would generally apply to most quality outdoor learning experiences, as we currently understand them. There are a few exceptions, however, which stand out and make Forest School different from, for instance, the daily outdoor experience of an early years setting. These are:

- the role of place;
- the role of the adult as facilitator of children's learning;
- training.

The first main difference is the *place* where Forest School occurs. This is usually a dedicated and exclusive site which can be in the school grounds, but is only used for the Forest School experience. Because this space is only used for the Forest School experience and is frequently returned to, it becomes a special place to be together as a group and to interact with what is around. Although many of the skills can be transferred to daily outdoor practice in settings, they cannot replace the special quality of the Forest School site. My own experience as a practitioner bears this out. Having visited Sweden in 2004 and observed the *I Ur och Skur* (Rain or Shine) outdoor settings in the forest, my own practice was transformed. Each week, for one half-day session, we visited a small wood just ten minutes' walking distance from the setting. The place became very special and familiar to the children and families. The children wore appropriate clothing, carried their own rucksack containing a drink, snack and mat. We walked, talked, sang, played and picnicked for the session. (See Figure 8.1 for more information on this.) We were able to do this for the whole year, regardless of the weather. My observations of the impact of *place* on learning were borne out in the developing confidence and self-esteem of all the children. Rules were special to the space and rarely broken. The strong sense of being a community, sharing this magical space together alongside the creatures and plants that lived there, fostered cohesion within the group. It also developed a sense of the interdependence between man and nature. For a fuller picture of this experience see *Playing Outside Rain or Shine* (Joyce 2006).

The second main difference is *the role of the adult* in Forest School. Knight (2009) and Murray (2003) argue that the success of the Forest School in the UK

Figure 8.1 Through rhyme and song the group learn about features of their Forest School environment, in this case the ash tree in winter

is dependent on good communication between schools and Forest School leaders. Falch-Lovesey et al. (2005), in their Norfolk-based research on the impact of the Forest School on learning, argue for the need to make connections between the curriculum and outdoor learning. While agreeing in principle I would urge a note of caution. From a Foucauldian perspective it has to be seen that Forest School, as with mainstream education and policy, brings into play power relations between individuals or groups, whether of children or adults. Unless the facilitative rather than coercive role of the adult outside is fully understood and valued, the curriculum outcome-led approach to learning so prevalent in our settings today will dilute the huge benefits to be gained from the Forest School experience. This facilitative, Vygotskian approach to 'scaffolding' child-centred learning, where the tasks are broken down into manageable chunks as noted in Knight's list of generic qualities in Forest School, is an essential ingredient. Being aware of one's own practice, and the power over others that is always involved in this, is a lesson in fact to be drawn from Foucault, who is interested in much more than coercion and discipline alone. What he was most interested in was identifying our own inevitable involvement in relations of power so that we could examine our own freedom better (Joyce 2003).

The third main difference is that specific accredited *training* is a requirement for all Forest School leaders and advisable for assistants. This is seen as crucial in promoting child-centred learning with adults as facilitators in that learning. No such training happens in mainstream practice regarding outdoor learning. Activities and resources to deliver curriculum objectives are often described but little discussion of the approach to learning takes place. Practitioners generally take their indoor teacher-led methods outside, largely because the outdoor space is not valued for its pedagogical opportunities for learning. Maynard and Waters' (2007) concern for the practitioners' view that the outdoors is not connected to their primary task as educators to deliver curriculum raises many questions. This is a clear illustration of the urgent need for an understanding of and training in pedagogy – a theory of teaching – which would create the necessary self-awareness for good practice. The Forest School addresses this issue head-on in its training process, which has a clear, well-defined pedagogy. Waite and Rea (2006) fear that tying Forest School pedagogy into a national, prescriptive curriculum could potentially suppress opportunities in the outdoors for creativity and imaginative thinking. Davis (1998) argues that environmental education should play a central role in all outdoor learning so that children can begin to get to grips with notions of sustainability. My only fear regarding the use of this approach is that practitioners may see the weekly trip to Forest School for a six-week period as satisfying the tick-box requirements of the curriculum regarding outdoor learning. Rather than taking back the essential qualities and methodologies observed in Forest School and applying these to their own outdoor practice reflectively, they are in danger of leaving the outdoors to the 'professionals'.

Maynard (2007b) suggests that Forest School is really an old idea which has been reshaped to suit current lifestyles and curriculum demands. The main aims and ethos of the Forest School approach to learning sit well, in her view, alongside the philosophy of earlier pioneers such as Isaacs and McMillan. I would go further and include Comenius, Pestalozzi, Froebel and Frohm in this list.

Reflective questions

Consider the following questions individually or in a group:

- Murray (2003) identified 'enjoyment by teachers and leaders' as a critical success factor generic to a thriving Forest School. What part does 'enjoyment' play in our current EYFS for practitioners?
- Is enjoyment, in your view, a significant feature of good practice?

9 Conclusion

Even though the figures studied have distinctive differences, several common themes have strongly emerged so far. Although these themes are closely inter-linked it seems appropriate to discuss them individually. They are:

- war and persecution, and the role of religion and the state in this;
- utopianism and the natural world;
- loss, personal and public: of family, identity;
- the central role of the mother and the family;
- the growth of teaching as a profession and education as a science.

War and persecution

This stands out as the strongest theme uniting all the pioneers. Comenius and Pestalozzi spent most of their lives on the move, persecuted by church and state for their religious and political ideals. The failed revolutions of 1848 created fear and suspicion in the minds of the Prussian government, which issued its *Kindergarten Verbot*, anathemizing Froebel's individualist approach to learning as a threat to national security. Pestalozzi and Froebel's educational philosophy can be seen as a response to the chaos of war. McMillan responded to state concerns regarding the nation's health after the Boer War, and her child-saving work continued throughout the hardship of two World Wars. Froebel and Frohm were both in the military during wartime and this powerfully influenced their vision of change, and an emphasis on peace and co-operation is integral to the ethos of *Skogsmulle, I Ur och Skur* and the Forest Schools.

Utopianism

This theme is closely related to that of war and persecution. All the pioneers sought and believed there was a better world to be created, and practitioners saw education as the key to this. Comenius lived in an age when utopian thinking was at its height. In the midst of war and destruction, and in the context of the search for new scientific understandings of the world, religion slowly ceased to be the main source of authority in educational thinking. Pestalozzi sought a better world in America, which was long a source of utopian hopes, while Froebel and McMillan understood the garden to be the interface of peace and chaos. All looked to the natural world as a model for their practice. Frohm aspired to a future where the earth's natural resources were not under threat and sought to bring this about through educating the very young child to respect environmental sustainability. The Forest School approach can be seen as reaching back to the world of nature with all its healing, therapeutic powers so as to counter our highly technological, highly regulated lives.

Loss: personal and public

Again this third theme is linked to war, persecution and a desire to create a better world. Comenius, Pestalozzi, Froebel and McMillan all lost a parent when they were very young. Comenius's personal losses continued with the untimely death of his wife and children, and then the death of his second wife. He was publicly humiliated by having his books burned and lost many of his manuscripts, as well as the right to remain in his homeland. Pestalozzi and Froebel lost public favour owing to the growing conservatism of the state, something which itself followed a period of war. McMillan's greatest loss in later life was the death of her sister Rachel. All these pioneers saw a move back to the harmony of nature as a model for a good life and as a way of redeeming the losses they had suffered. This might be personal losses, or the perception that the world was losing its essential value, especially the rational world in the face of an increasingly technological society. Frohm and the Forest School approach shared this latter vision, most of all the loss of nature.

The central role of the mother and the family

The mother emerges as central to the success of all learning approaches advocated by these pioneers. In the case of Comenius and Froebel, this emphasis can be attributed, in large part, to the loss of their own mothers when they were very young. Comenius gives the role of early childhood education back to the mother as the first educator, viewing the role of the father as a supportive one. Froebel's later work with very young children focused almost exclusively on female practitioners. The prominence given to mothers in the work of Pestalozzi and McMillan was owed to the early death of their fathers. Pestalozzi portrays the family living space as the place where all meaningful learning begins and tried to recreate this at Stans. Like Froebel, McMillan sought to educate mothers and raise their status as the first educators. Frohm involved and supported mothers in their drive to create a better future for their children. All saw the family as the most significant support of early learning.

The growth of teaching as a profession and education as a science

From the time of Comenius to the present day, education has evolved as a professional activity, one marked by the fluctuating status of its practitioners. Comenius, Pestalozzi and Froebel all despised the harsh, meaningless teaching methods they were subjected to and worked at creating systems which would engage children, using meaningful, first-hand and sensory experiences. Teaching had for long depended on voluntary bodies which were generally dominated by organized religion. The advent of mass schooling in Britain in 1870 dramatically changed this situation and, as the government became more and more involved, the church became sidelined. State intervention and regulation eventually led to higher status and pay for teachers in the early twentieth century, when training became more highly regulated. As new theories of psychology and sociology emerged, education came increasingly to be viewed as a 'science', complete with its own institutions (for example, schools of education, university departments, learned journals, professional certification and so on). McMillan was central to these developments, bringing together the education and medical welfare of children as prerequisites for a 'healthy' adulthood. In Sweden similar changes were taking place. The Swedish Lutheran Church dominated practice until the nineteenth-century adoption of Parliamentary democratic reform, which strongly influenced the future practice and status of teachers. The major difference was that this reform operated at a municipal rather than a central level.

A study of the history of early childhood and outdoor learning enables us to ask different questions. Taking a step back and applying a social and historical perspective on pedagogy frees the mind from current policy and its impact on practice. It enables a fresh look at things often taken for granted, as if somehow these have always been there. This is most of all evident in the common perception that 'childhood' is a natural state and has always existed. As we have seen, there was a time when 'childhood' was entirely unknown. Indeed, it does not exist in large parts of the world today. And 'childhood' itself has constantly changed historically. Accepting that 'taken for granted' notions have shaped our formation requires a step back so that seemingly 'new' initiatives can be fully explored, their origins understood and the major factors which influenced them discovered (Vincent 2008). James Vernon has strongly argued for the necessity of the historical perspective:

> [By] examining the historical processes that have bound us together in our diversity . . . we can understand what we hold in common and what we do not. History teaches us that nothing lasts for ever, that what appears natural and normal to us may have been strange or even abhorrent to preceding generations.
>
> (Vernon 2010)

'New' approaches to learning do not, therefore, appear in a vacuum. They are the product of what has gone before. The current promotion of the outdoors in statutory government documentation needs to be viewed in the long-term historical perspective, the one outlined in this book.

All of the pioneers had a view of children being part of, not separate or distinct from, nature. All of them have shown us the way forward, towards a better education which involves the entirety of the child's experience, and which treats all children as equal. Their ideas are of real importance to us at this time, a time when inequality is a powerful factor in children's lives and when the destruction of nature is a prime concern. What they have to say to us about children's physical, emotional and intellectual needs is every bit as relevant today as it was in their own time. Their emphasis on quality, on caring for and loving the child as the essential foundation for future learning, simply cannot be ignored. What needs to be done to enable caring for and loving the child once again to be a priority? The pioneers learned these lessons from their observations of nature and its processes. These are simple lessons, in essence, but is it possible now to step back from constantly being told how to be with children and have faith in our own experience-based observations of what their needs really are? For instance, can an understanding of 'readiness' drawn from the natural world (for example, 'readiness' to flower, and 'readiness' to move on to the next stage) inform our practice regarding when and how to teach young child to read and be numerate? Is it possible to step back and wait until the child is ready to understand abstract concepts of letter sounds and symbols, for instance, rather than pushing forward regardless, because that is what the documentation prescribes? Can nature teach us the way forward to a more caring, loving world, in the way the pioneers believed it could? This broad and generous view of education which includes love and well-being can greatly help us in our understanding of children's needs and of a pedagogy that meets their needs.

The legacy of these great pioneers is also their devotion, commitment and courage, courage evident often in the face of persecution and serious loss.

There is little doubt that the same level of dedication exists today, since everyone, generally speaking, wants to do the best for children in their care. Those who, in the model of the pioneers, seek more 'holistic' and 'natural' methods of educating children often share the same experience as the people studied here, namely the opposition of entrenched interest and traditional, supposedly 'time-honoured' ways of doing things (when it is obvious that time does not in fact 'honour ' them at all). However, it is important to understand that all activities involved in decision making involve power and therefore one's own responsibility and self-examination, whether this involves setting up a Nature School or deciding how to organize literacy activities in a reception class. Without being able to distance oneself historically and become critically self-aware, understanding and development is unlikely to take place. In order to develop one's own practice it is most important to understand how power is exercised. What sort of power relations govern practice, the practice of others, and of oneself? One's own practice, so understood, can then help obviate the deleterious effects of so much present-day practice. (These ideas would have been so helpful to Pestalozzi at Yverdun. As he distanced himself from practice to concentrate on his writing, he failed to notice how the relationships of power between his teachers, which had hitherto been a strength of the school, now became highly problematic.) Being critically aware and closely monitoring oneself should not stop innovative practice, however. On the contrary, it should empower one to be more innovative.

What is it to be a good citizen environmentally? Surely, as we are all children of nature, as in the Swedish model, this should involve greater equality? This in turn should mean a developed pedagogy for the early years with particular emphasis on the skills of peace and co-operation, as experienced in a democratic commitment to and experience of the outdoor environment? With governments' increasing concern with the environment, it is clear that outdoor learning will be more and more important politically. It is necessary for practitioners and all interested parties to be part of this political movement, making sure that the lessons of the great pioneering figures here are properly learned, and brought to all children in a democratic and equal fashion.

Therefore, to conclude, I agree wholeheartedly with Dighe's concern that, 'One can hardly imagine a generation of persons with neither interest in, or knowledge of the outdoors making responsible decisions regarding the environment' (1993: 62).

Bibliography

Abbott, L. and Gillen, J. (2000) 'Put the baby genius kits in the bin': what did the geniuses say? Paper presented at the annual meeting of the European Conference on Quality in Early Childhood Education (EECERA). London, 29 August–1 September 2000.

Akdag, R. and Danzon, M. (2006) *Diet and Physical Activity for Health*. Geneva: World Health Organization.

Alvestad, M. and Samuelsson, I. (1999) A comparison of the national preschool curricula in Norway and Sweden, *Early Childhood Research and Practice*, 1(2): 1–17.

Anning, A. (1998) Appropriateness or effectiveness of the early childhood curriculum in the UK: some research evidence, *International Journal of Early Years Education*, 6(3): pp 299–314.

Ariès, P. (1962) *Centuries of Childhood*. Harmondsworth: Penguin Books.

Bai, L. (2005) Children at play: a childhood beyond the Confucian shadow, *Childhood*, 12(9): 9–32.

Banks, F. and Schofield, J. (2005) *Nature's Playground. Activities, Crafts and Games to Encourage Children to Get Outdoors*. London: Frances Lincoln.

Bilton, H. (2004) *Playing Outside. Activities, Ideas and Inspiration for the Early Years*. London: David Fulton Publishers.

Blanning, T. (2000) *The Oxford History of Modern Europe*. Oxford: Oxford University Press.

Board of Education (1905) *Report on Children Under Five Years of Age in Public Elementary Schools*. London: Her Majesty's Stationery Office.

Bond, S. (2005) *Why Do Forest Schools?* http://www.greenlighttrust.org/The%20 Full20%Story.htm. Accessed 4 September 2009.

Bond, S. (2007) Forest School: relational pedagogy in action. Paper presented at Anglia Ruskin University conference: Reclaiming Relational Pedagogy in Early Childhood: Learning from International Experience, Cambridge, 19–21 April.

Boucher, L. (1982) *Tradition and Change in Swedish Education*. Oxford: Pergamon Press.

Bowen, J. (1981) Volume. *A History of Western Education. The Modern West Europe and the New World* (Volume 3). London: Methuen and Co.

Bradburn, E. (1989) *Margaret McMillan. Portrait of a Pioneer*. London: Routledge.

Breiting, S. and Wickenberg, P. (2010) The progressive development of environmental education in Sweden and Denmark, *Environmental Education Research*, 16(1): 1, 9–37.

Browne, N. (2004) *Gender Equity in the Early Years.* Maidenhead: Open University Press.

Canfield, A. (1965) Folk high schools in Denmark and Sweden: a comparative analysis, *Comparative Education Review,* 9(1): 18–24.

Capkova, D. (1970) The recommendations of Comenius regarding the education of young children, in C.H. Dobinson (ed.) *UNESCO: Commemoration of Tercentenary of Death of Comenius. Comenius and Contemporary Education. An International Symposium.* Hamburg: UNESCO, pp. 17–33.

Capkova, D. and Frijhoff, W. (1992) Jan Amos Comenius, 1592–1670. An introduction, *Pedagogica Historica,* 28(2): 175–83.

Chen, X. (2003) 'Cultivating children as you would valuable plants': the gardening governmentality of child saving, Toronto, Canada, 1880s–1920s, *Journal of Historical Sociology,* 16(4): 460–86.

Clauser, J. (1961) Comenius considers discipline, *Peabody Journal of Education,* 39(1): 50–3.

Comenius, J. (1998) *The Labyrinth of the World and the Paradise of the Heart,* translated by Howard Louthan and Andrea Sterk. New York: Paulist Press.

Comenius, J. (2009) *The School of Infancy: An Essay on the Education of Youth during their First Six Years: To Which is Prefixed a Sketch of the Life of the Author.* Milton Keynes: Lightning Source UK.

Conran, T. and Pearson, D. (1998) *The Essential Garden Book.* London: Conran Octopus Limited.

Corsaro, W. (1997) *The Sociology of Childhood.* Thousand Oaks, CA: Pine Forge Press.

Cunningham, H. (1995) *Children and Childhood in Western Society since 1500.* London: Longman.

Cunningham, H. (2006) *The Invention of Childhood.* London: BBC Books.

Curtis, S. (1948) *History of Education in Great Britain,* 4th edition. Foxton: University Tutorial Press.

David, T. and Powell, S. (1999) Changing childhoods. Changing minds, in T. David (ed.) *Young Children Learning.* London: Paul Chapman Publishers/Sage Publications.

Davis, B., Rea, T. and Waite, S. (2006) The special nature of the outdoors: its contribution to the education of children aged 3–11, *Australian Journal of Outdoor Education,* 10(2): 3–12.

Davis, J. (1998) Young children, environmental education, and the future, *Early Childhood Education Journal,* 26(2): 117–23.

DCSF (Department for Children, Schools and Families) (2007a) *Primary National Strategy. Confident, Capable and Creative: Supporting Boys' Achievements. Guidance for Practitioners in the Early Years Foundation Stage.* London: DCSF Publications.

DCSF (2007b) *Primary National Strategy. Supporting Children Learning English as an Additional Language. Guidance for Practitioners in the Early Years Foundation Stage.* London: DCSF Publications.

DCSF (2007c) *Children's Plan.* London: DCSF Publications.

DCSF (2008) *Staying Safe Action Plan. Cross-government Strategy for Improving Children and Young People's Safety*. London: DCSF Publications.

DCSF and DCMS (Department for Culture, Media and Sport) (2008) *The Play Strategy*. London: DCSF Publications.

De Mause, L. (1974) The evolution of childhood, in L. de Mause (ed.) *History of Childhood*. New York: Harper and Row, pp. 1–74.

Derry, T. (1979) *A History of Scandinavia. Norway, Sweden, Denmark, Finland and Iceland*. Minneapolis, MN: University of Minnesota Press.

DES (Department of Education and Science) (1990) *Starting with Quality: Report of the Committee of Enquiry into the Quality of Educational Experience Offered to Three and Four Year Olds* (Rumbold Report). London: HMSO.

DFEE (Department for Education and Employment) and SCAA (School Curriculum and Assessment Authority) (1996) *Desirable Outcomes for Children's Learning*. London: HMSO.

DfES (Department for Education and Skills) (2002) *Birth to Three Matters: A Framework to Support Children in their Earliest Years*. London: DfES.

DfES (2003a) *Excellence and Enjoyment. A Strategy for Primary Schools*. Nottingham: DfES.

DfES (2003b) *Every Child Matters: Change for Children*. Green Paper. London: The Stationery Office.

DfES (2003c) *National Standards for Under-eights Day Care and Childminding*. London: DfES.

DfES (2003d) *Sure Start Guidance 2004–2006: Overview and Local Delivery Arrangements*. London: DfES.

DfES (2006a) *Learning Outside the Classroom Manifesto*. Nottingham: DfES.

DfES (2006b) *Schools for the Future. Designing School Grounds*. Norwich: The Stationery Office.

DfES (2007a) *Early Years Foundation Stage*. Nottingham: DfES.

DfES (2007b) *Letters and Sounds: Principles and Practice of High-quality Phonics. Six-phase Teaching Programme*. Nottingham: DfES.

Dighe, J. (1993) Children and the earth, *Young Children*, 48(3): 58–63. Cited in J. Davis (1998) Young children, environmental education, and the future, *Early Childhood Education Journal*, 26(2): 117–23.

Donovan, M. and Fiske, T. (with Beardsley, J. and Kemp, M.) (2010) *The Andy Goldsworthy Project*. London: Thames and Hudson.

DuCharme, C.C. (1992) Margaret McMillan and Maria Montessori: champions of the poor. Paper presented at the annual meeting of the National Association for the Education of Young Children, New Orleans, 12–15 November.

Düring, I. (1951) *The Swedish School-reform 1950. A Summary of the Government Bill at the Request of the 1946 School Commission*. Upsalla: Appelbergs Poktryckeriaktiebolag.

Edgington, M. (2002) *The Great Outdoors*. London: Early Education.

Elliott, B. (1986) *Victorian Gardens*. London: B.T. Batsford.

Elwell-Sutton, L. (n.d.) *A History of Kibbo Kift.* http://www.kibbokift.org/kkkhist. html. Accessed 19 July 2010.

Environmental Education Forum (2008) Playboard: fit for play award, *Little Leef: The Newsletter of the Environmental Education Forum,* 6(2): 1–11.

Falch-Lovesey, S., Lord, C. and Ambrose, L. (2005) *Forest Schools in Norfolk: Pilot Study Report and Evaluation.* Norwich: Norfolk County Council.

Faubion, J. (ed.) (1994) *Michel Foucault. Power: Essential Works of Foucault 1954– 1984,* Volume 3, 4th edition, translated by R. Hurley and others. London: Allen Lane, Penguin Press.

Forest Education Initiative (FEI) (2009) *Background to FEI Forest Schools.* http://www. foresteducation.org/forest_schools.php?=4. Accessed 30 September 2010.

Friluftsfrämjandet (2010) *Friluftsfrämjandets Skogsmulle Prinsessa.* http://www. Friluftsfrämjandet.se/guest/hem. Accessed 19 June 2010.

Frohm, A. (2010a) Recorded interview with Anna Frohm in Sweden in possession of author. Lidingö, August.

Frohm, G. (1970) *Skogsmulle.* Stockholm: P.A. Norstedt and Söners förlag.

Frohm, G. (1971) *Skogsmulle och Fjällfina. Natursagor för barn.* Stockholm: P.A. Norstedt and Söners förlag.

Frohm, G. (1978) *Laxe, Skogsmulle van i vattnen.* Stockholm: Rabén and Sjörgrens förlag.

Frohm, G. (1997) *Nova. Skogsmulle van Irymden.* Stockholm: Friluftsfrämjandet.

Frohm, S. (2010b) Telephone communication with Sten Frohm: notes in possession of author. Lidingö, August.

Frost, S. (1966) *History and Philosophy of Western Education.* Columbus, OH: Charles Merrill Books Inc.

Fuller, B. (2007) (with Bridges, M. and Pai, S.) *Standarized Childhood. The Political and Cultural Struggle over Early Education.* Palo Alto, CA: Stanford University Press.

Garrick, R. (2009) *Playing Outdoors in the Early Years,* 2nd edition. London: Continuum International Publishing Group.

Goldson, B. (1997) 'Childhood': an introduction to historical and theoretical analyses, in P. Scraton (ed.) *Childhood in Crisis?* London: UCL Press.

Graffman, H. (2010) Recorded interview in Sweden, in possession of author. *Friluftsfrämjandet* headquarters, Stockholm, August.

Gutek, G. (1972) *A History of Western Educational Experience.* Chicago, IL: Loyola University.

Guter, H. (2010) Recorded interview in Sweden, in possession of author. *Friluftsfrämjandet* headquarters, Stockholm, August.

Hanawalt, B. (1993) *Growing Up in Medieval London. The Experience of Childhood in History.* Oxford: Oxford University Press.

Hannon, C., Wood, C. and Bazalgette, L. (2010). *In Loco Parentis.* London: Demos.

Hansard (1884), Sir Charles Lewis, Parliamentary Committee, 16 May. http://hansard. millbanksystems.com/commons/1884/May/16/committee-progress-6th- hay-second-night#S3V0288P0_18840516_HOC_86. Accessed 5 May 2011.

Harrison, J. (1969) *Robert Owen and the Owenites in Britain and America. The Quest for the New Moral World.* London: Routledge and Kegan Paul.

Hart, C. (1998) *Doing a Literature Review. Releasing the Social Science Research Imagination.* London: Sage Publications.

Hayward, F. (1904) *The Educational Ideas of Pestalozzi and Froebel.* London: Ralph Holland and Co.

Heafford, M. (1967) *Pestalozzi. His Thought and its Relevance Today.* London: Methuen and Co.

Hedlund, M. (1997) *En smula Gösta,* DVD translated by Magnus Linde. Mirakel Film and TV AB 1999-08-644 75 00.

Herrington, S. (2001) Kindergarten: garden pedagogy from romanticism to reform, *Landscape Journal,* 20(1–01): 30–47.

Heywood, C. (2001) *A History of Childhood: Children and Childhood in the West from Mediaeval to Modern Times.* Cambridge: Polity Press.

Hinton, R. (2008) Children's participation and good governance: limitations of the theoretical literature, *International Journal of Children's Rights,* 16: 285–300.

HMT (Her Majesty's Treasury) (2004) *Choice for Parents, the Best Start for Children: A Ten-year Strategy for Childcare.* London: The Stationery Office.

Hobhouse, P. (2002) *The Story of Gardening.* London: Dorling Kindersley.

Hope, G., Austin, R., Dismore, H., Hammond, S. and Whyte, T. (2007) Wild woods or urban jungle: playing it safe or freedom to roam, *Education 3–13,* 35(4): 321–32.

Husen, T. (2003) Comenius and Sweden, and Begt Skytte's Sopholis, *Scandinavian Journal of Educational Research,* 47(4): 387–98.

James, A. and James, A.L. (eds) (2008) *European Childhoods. Cultures, Politics and Childhoods in Europe.* Basingstoke: Palgrave Macmillan.

Jenkinson, S. (2001) *The Genius of Play. Celebrating the Spirit of Childhood.* Stroud: Hawthorn Press.

Johansson, I. (1997) The interplay between organization and pedagogic content: results from a study reflecting the changes within 12 pre-schools in Stockholm during a three-year period, *European Early Childhood Education Research Journal,* 5(2): 33–46.

Johnson, B. (2009) GPS wristwatch helps parents track children, *Guardian,* 12 January.

Josefsson, E. (2010) Telephone communication with Eva Josefsson: notes in possession of author. Lidingö, August.

Joyce, P. (2003) *The Rule of Freedom.* London: Verso.

Joyce, R. (2006) *Playing Outside Rain or Shine.* Blackburn: Educational Printing Services.

Kent, N. (2008) *A Concise History of Sweden.* Cambridge: Cambridge University Press.

Knight, S. (2009) *Forest Schools and Outdoor Learning in the Early Years.* London: Sage Publications.

Kwon, Y. (2002) Changing curriculum for early childhood education in England, *Early Childhood Research and Practice Journal,* Fall: 1–11.

Læesøe, J. and Öhman, J. (2010) The meaning of democracy and values in environmental and sustainable education – contributions from Danish and Swedish research. *Environmental Education Research* (special issue), 16(1).

Lawrence, E. (ed.) (1952) *Frederich Froebel and English Education*. London: Routledge and Kegan Paul.

Liebschner, J. (1991) *Foundations of Progressive Education. The History of the Froebel Society*. Cambridge: The Lutterworth Press.

Linde, S. (2010a) The *skogsmulle* concept. Unpublished paper. http://www.friluftsframjandet.se/skogsmullestiftelsen/32. Accessed 5 October.

Linde, S. (2010b) *Start av I Ur och Skur* (The start of 'In rain or shine'). Unpublished paper. http://www.friluftsframjandet.se/skogsmullestiftelsen/32. Accessed 5 October.

Löfdahl, A. and Prieto, H.P. (2009) Institutional narratives within the performative pre-school in Sweden: 'If we write that we're no good, that's not good publicity!', *Early Years*, 29(3): 261–70.

Louv, R. (2008) *Last Child in the Woods. Saving our Children from Nature-deficit Disorder*, 2nd edition. Chapel Hill, NC: Algonquin Books.

Lowndes, G. (1960) *The Children's Champion*. London: Museum Press.

McMillan, M. (1919) *The Nursery School*. London: J.M. Dent & Sons.

McMillan, M. (1927) *The Life of Rachel McMillan*. London: J.M. Dent & Sons.

MacNaughton, G. (2005) *Doing Foucault in Early Childhood Studies. Applying Poststructural Ideas*. London: Routledge.

Magnergard, O. (1999) *Dödsfall. Gösta Frohm*, translated by Magnus Linde. *Svenska Dagbladet*, 30 September.

Malone, K. (2008) *Every Experience Matters: An Evidence-based Research Report on the Role of Learning Outside the Classroom for Children's Whole Development from Birth to Eighteen Years*. Report commissioned by Farming and Countryside Education for UK Department for Children, Schools and Families, Wollongong, Australia.

Mayer, F. (1960) *A History of Educational Thought*, 2nd edition. Columbus, OH: Charles Merrill Books Inc.

Maynard, T. (2007a) Encounters with Forest School and Foucault: a risky business?, *Education 3–13*, 35(4): 379–91.

Maynard, T. (2007b) Forest schools in Great Britain: an initial exploration, *Contemporary Issues in Early Childhood*, 8(4): 320–31.

Maynard, T. and Waters, J. (2007) Learning in the outdoor environment. A missed opportunity? *Early Years*, 27(3): 255–65.

Montessori, M. (1966) *The Secret of Childhood*, translated by M. Joseph Costelloe. New York: Ballantine Books.

Moss, P. (2007) Bringing politics into the nursery: early childhood education as a democratic practice. Working paper 43. The Hague: Bernard van Leer Foundation.

Moss, P. (2009) There are alternatives! Markets and democratic experimentalism in early childhood education and care. Working paper in Early Childhood Development. The Hague: Bernard van Leer Foundation.

Mukerjii, C. (1997) *Territorial Ambitions and the Gardens of Versailles*. Cambridge: Cambridge University Press.

Murray, R. (2003) *Forest School Evaluation Project*. London: New Economics Foundation.

Newberry, S. (2008) Economic and social policy tensions: early childhood education and care in a marketised environment. Working paper. Sydney: University of Sydney.

Nielsen, R. (2008) Children and nature: cultural ideas and social practices in Norway, in A. James and A.L. James (eds) (2008) *European Childhoods. Cultures, Politics and Childhoods in Europe*. Basingstoke: Palgrave Macmillan.

Norden (2009) *Environment Prize to Swedish Forest Schools*, November. http://www.norden.org/en/news-and-events/news/environment-prize-to-swedish-forest-schools. Accessed 21 October 2009.

Nordkvelle, Y. (2000) The idea of method in teaching and doing research. A postcolonial view on the roots of educational theory after Pierre de la Ramee (1515–1572). Paper presented at the European Conference on Educational Research, Edinburgh, 20–23 September.

Norfolk Schools (2010). *Case Studies*. http://www.norfolk.gov.uk/myportal/index.cfm?s=1&m=1654&p=1128,index. Accessed 4 November 2010.

Nutbrown, C. (2006) *Key Concepts in Early Childhood Education and Care*. London: Sage Publications.

Nyström, L.H. (1913) *Ellen Key: Her Life and Work*, translated from the Swedish by A.E.B. Fries. New York: The Knickerbocker Press. Reprint from the collections of the University of Michigan Library.

O'Brien, L. and Murray, R. (2007) Forest Schools and its impacts on young children: case studies in Britain, *Urban Forestry & Greening*, 6: 249–65.

OECD (Organization for Economic Cooperation and Development) (1981) *Reviews of National Policies for Education. Educational Reforms in Sweden*. Paris: OECD.

O'Hara, K. (2007) *Education Issues: Weblog. 'Children are being reared in captivity.'* http://news.bbc.co.uk/1/hi/education/6720661.stm. Accessed 27 March 2009.

Oppenheim, C. and Lawton, K. (2009) The fight to end child poverty. Governing a world city. http//:www.ippr.org/articles/?id=3388. Accessed 26 February 2009.

Ouvry, M. (2003) *Exercising Muscles and Minds. Outdoor Play and the Early Years Curriculum*. London: National Children's Bureau.

Panek, J. (1991) *Comenius: Teacher of Nations*. Prague: Vychodoslovenske vydavatelstvo, Kosice, Orbis.

Pence, A. and Nsamenang, B. (2008) A case for early childhood development in sub-Saharan Africa. Working papers in early childhood development. The Hague: Bernard van Leer Foundation.

Perry, J. (2001) *Outdoor Play. Teaching Strategies with Young Children*. New York: Teachers College Press.

Pestalozzi, J.H. (1907) *How Gertrude Teaches Her Children: An Attempt to Help Mothers to Teach Their Own Children*, 4th edition. Translated by L.E. Holland and F.C. Turner. London: Swan, Sonnenschein and Co.

Plowden Report (1967) *Children and their Primary Schools*. A report of the Central Advisory Council for Education (England), 1. London: HMSO.

Porter, R. (2003) *Flesh in the Age of Reason. How the Enlightenment Transformed the Way We See our Bodies and Souls*. London: Penguin Books.

Postman, N. (1994) *The Disappearance of Childhood*. New York: Vintage Books.

Pound, L. (2005) *How Children Learn. From Montessori to Vygotsky-educational Theories and Approaches Made Easy*. Leamington Spa: Step Forward Publishing.

Pre-School Learning Alliance (2010) *A History of the Pre-School Learning Alliance*. http://www.pre-school.org.uk. Accessed 2 November 2010.

Pugh, G. (2006) The policy agenda for early childhood services, in G. Pugh and B. Duffy (eds) *Contemporary Issues in the Early Years*, 4th edition. London: Sage Publications.

Pugh, G. (2010) Improving outcomes for young children: can we narrow the gap? *Early Years*, 30(1): 5–14.

QCA (Qualifications and Curriculum Authority) (1999) *Early Learning Goals*. London: HMSO.

QCA (2000) *Curriculum Guidance for the Foundation Stage*. London: QCA.

Ranson, S. (1998) Lineages of the learning in society, in S. Ranson (ed.) *Inside the Learning Society*. London: Cassell, pp. 1–24.

Rickinson, M., Dillon, J., Teamey, K., Morris, M., Choi, M.Y., Sanders, D. and Benefield, P. (2004) *A Review of Research on Outdoor Learning*. Shrewsbury: Fields Study Council.

Roberts, J.M. (1996) *The Penguin History of Europe*. London: Penguin Books.

Robertson, J. (2008) *I ur och skur, 'rain or shine'. Swedish Forest Schools*. Report by Juliet Robertson, November. http://www.creativestarlearning.co.uk. Accessed 13 October 2010.

Roche, J. and Tucker, A. (2007) *Every Child Matters*: 'tinkering' or 'reforming' – an analysis of the development of the Children Act (2004) from an educational perspective, *Education 3–13*, 35(3): 213–23.

Rose, N. (1992) Towards a critical sociology of freedom. Inaugural lecture, Goldsmith's College, University of London, in P. Joyce (ed.) (1995) *Class*. Oxford: Oxford University Press.

Roth, A-C.V. and Månsson, A. (2009) Regulated childhood: equivalence with variation, *Early Years*, 29(2): 177–90.

Rousseau, J.J. (1780) *Emile*, translated by Barbara Foxley. London: J.M. Dent and Sons.

Sadler, J. (1966) *J.A. Comenius and the Concept of Universal Education*. London: George Allen and Unwin Ltd.

Sadler, J. (1970) Comenius as a man, in C.H. Dobinson (ed.) *UNESCO: Commemoration of Tercentenary of Death of Comenius. Comenius and Contemporary Education: An International Symposium*. Hamburg: UNESCO, pp. 9–16.

Scottish Government (2008) *The Early Years Framework*. Edinburgh: Scottish Government.

ScoutBaseUK (2010) *The History of Scouting*. http://www.scoutbase.org.uk/library/history. Accessed 4 November 2010.

Silber, K. (1973) *Pestalozzi. The Man and His Work*, 3rd edition. London: Routledge and Kegan Paul.

Simon, B. (1981) Why no pedagogy in England? in B. Simon and W. Taylor, *Education in the Eighties. The Central Issues*. London: Batsford Academic and Educational.

Skogsmulle Foundation (1999) *Goesta Frohm, 'ol'mulle', 1909–1999*. http://www.skogsmullestiftelsen.org/eng/frohm.htm. Accessed 23 October 2009.

Sköld, B. (2010) Recorded interview in Sweden, in possession of author. *Friluftsfrämjandet* headquarters, Stockholm, August.

Snicgoski, S. (1994) Froebel and early education in America, *Viewpoints*, 120: 1–15.

Spodek, B. (1988) Early childhood curriculum and the definition of knowledge. Paper presented at the Annual Conference of the American Educational Research Association, New Orleans, 5–9 April.

Steedman, C. (1990) *Childhood, Culture and Class in Britain: Margaret McMillan, 1860–1931*. London: Virago.

Stephen, C. (2010) Pedagogy: the silent partner in early years learning, *Early Years*, 30(1): 15–28.

Sylva, K., Melhuish, E., Sammons, P., Siraj-Blatchford, I. and Taggart, B. (2004) *The Effective Provision of Pre-school Education (EPPE) Project. Technical Paper 12 – The Final Report: Effective Pre-school Education*. London: DfES and Institute of Education, University of London.

Taylor, W. (1981) Contraction in context, in B. Simon and W. Taylor (eds) *Education in the Eighties. The Central Issues*. London: Batsford Academic and Educational.

Thomas, K. (1984) *Man and the Natural World. Changing Attitudes in England 1500–1800*. London: Penguin Books.

Thompson, F.M.L. (1990) (ed.) *The Cambridge History of Britain 1750–1950. Volume 3: Social Agencies and Institutions*. Cambridge: Cambridge University Press.

Tovey, H. (2007) *Playing Outdoors. Spaces and Places, Risk and Challenge*. Maidenhead: McGraw-Hill Open University Press.

Turner, J. (1972) The visual realism of Comenius, *History of Education*, 1(2): 113–38.

UN (United Nations) (1989) *Convention on the Rights of the Child*. New York: United Nations.

Valentine, G. (2004) *Public Space and the Cultured Childhood*. Aldershot: Ashgate Publishing.

Vernon, J. (2010) School history gets the TV treatment. Michael Gove is bringing in celebrities to revamp school history teaching, *Education Guardian,* 16 November. http://www.guardian.co.uk/education/2010/nov/16/school-history-gove-schama-tv/print. Accessed 18 November 2010.

Vincent, D. (2008) The end of literacy. Paper presented at History and Development Policy Workshop, Milton Keynes 7–8 April.

Waite, S. and Rea, T. (2006) Pedagogy or place? Attributed contributions of outdoor learning to creative teaching and learning. Paper presented at the British Educational Research Association annual conference, University of Warwick, 6–9 September.

Westermark, J. (2010) Recorded interview in Sweden, in possession of author. Lidingö, August.

Weston, P. (2000) *Friedrich Froebel: His Life, Times and Significance*. Roehampton: University of Surrey.

White, J. (1909) *The Educational Ideas of Froebel*. London: University Tutorial Press.

White, R. (2004) Young children's relationship with nature: its importance to children's development and the earth's future, *Taproot*, Fall/Winter, 16(2): 1–5.

Wilkinson, R. and Pickett, K. (2010) *The Spirit Level*. London: Penguin.

Wood, E. (2007) New directions in play: consensus or collision? *Education 3–13*, 35(4): 309–20.

Wyness, M. (2006) *Childhood and Society. An Introduction to the Sociology of Childhood*. Basingstoke: Palgrave Macmillan.

Zufiaurre, B. (2007) Education and schooling: from modernity to postmodernity, *Pedagogy, Culture and Society*, 15(2): 139–51.

Index

Printed in Poland
by Amazon Fulfillment
Poland Sp. z o.o., Wrocław

51331556R00083